# they
## took their
## Stand

# they took their Stand

### by
## Emma Gelders Sterne

Crowell-Collier Press, New York

Collier-Macmillan Limited, London

PICTURE CREDITS: Black Star, 142; The Library Company of Philadelphia, 19; Historical Pictures Service, 34, 49, 60–61, 68–69, 72–73, 79, 106, 113, 120; United Press International, 150–151, 196, 220–221; West Point Museum Collection, U.S. Army Signal Corps Photographs, 99; Wide World Photos, 153, 191, 202–203, 207, 212, 215.

To Joseph Gelders: 1898–1950

He brought changes into a world
that resents change, and yet
found time, in quiet places, to
listen to the future.

# Preface

I do not know how it is with other writers, but for myself the idea, the plan, the characters, even the last line of a book are generally complete in my mind before I begin to write. There remains only the slow, tedious hours of putting words down on paper. It has not been so with this book about the role of white Southerners on Southern soil who took their stand by the side of the Negro people. This book has been twenty years in growing and has changed in form and content and is for me "unfinished business" still.

During the years I was growing up in Alabama, I never heard a white Southern defender of Negro rights mentioned by name. Even after I had come, through reading and through experience in New England and New York, to some knowledge of the black Americans' never-ceasing struggle for equal citizenship, I assumed that any white allies they had were from the North. I thought that merely to perceive the tragic situation in the Southern states, where the vast majority of the Negro people then lived, required the perspective of distance. I pitied the "silent South," explaining to myself that to act in isolation and against "self-interest" and social pressures was too much to ask of ordinary people. There was Thomas Jefferson, of course, but look how he had been driven to compromise his anti-slavery position! Jefferson appeared to me a unique example and he had died, an old man, still a slaveholder, confessing failure.

John Fairfield's part in the Underground Railroad in the years before the Civil War moved me greatly. But his role in leading slaves to freedom was overshadowed by Harriet Tubman, William Still and the other famous Negro "conductors." Nevertheless, as a white Southerner I felt a special interest when I read about Fairfield in Henrietta Buckmaster's *Let My People Go,* and I considered using Fairfield as a sort of Robin Hood hero for a novel—a white Virginian from a slave-owning family, leading slaves to Canada!

John Fairfield's true significance was not clear to me until I took a course in Negro History under Dr. Herbert Aptheker and came to understand the gaping hole in the fabric of American history as it was taught—and for the most part is still taught today—in our public schools and colleges. The flight of almost a hundred thousand men and women and children from slavery is only part of that untold history. The role played by a few white Southerners in that era is only one segment. I saw that telling the romantic story of one brave man in one era was not what was needed.

I began doing some research. John Laurens came to my attention through a footnote in a biography of George Washington by Douglas Southall Freeman; Sophia Auld's story leaped out of the pages of slave-born Frederick Douglass' autobiography, which I had read several times before. As an old suffragette, I knew the name Angelina Grimké long before I became aware of her key role in the abolition movement.

Meanwhile there appeared the painstaking study by a young South Carolinian, *The Mind of the South.* When J. W. Cash, the author, overwhelmed by the criticism his honest work met from fellow Southerners, shot himself, I realized that the tradition of dissent was not dead and not without its sacrifices. And here was my brother, Joe Gelders, in Alabama, who deserved a chapter in the book I was by then determined to undertake—a chapter I found myself unable to write because he *was* my brother. His full story is only one of the many omissions caused by the need to choose a few representatives from the many men and women who over the years have "endured the slings of outrageous fortune for conscience sake."

Their actions had small part in changing history. No statues have been raised to commemorate their deeds and words. Their names are not engraved on bronze tablets. Casual mention in memoires, old newspaper reports, a few published biographies or autobiographical volumes, notably Anne Braden's *The Wall Between* and Cedric Belfrage's book on Claude Williams have been my printed sources.

Even in the case of Claude Williams and Anne Braden the reference books have been supplemented by personal contact with the people themselves and their friends. It has been my good fortune to know most of those who have stayed in the Southern fields of work in later years, and I have enlisted their help in many ways.

The Reverend Dunbar Ogden and Bob Zellner are the exceptions. The detailed account of Ogden's experience in Little Rock is, however, based on his own story told to Anne Braden and related to me with permission to use the material as I have set it down. Letters and tape recordings sent me by Bob Zellner during the crucial period of his work in the Freedom Movement, 1960–1965, enabled me to give his story almost in his own words.

Finally, I am indebted to Herbert Jones of San José for access to the original source of the Fairfield saga: Levi Coffin's memories of the days of the Underground Railroad as dictated to his niece, Mr. Jones's mother. This rare, out-of-print document was read by my daughter and sometime collaborator, Barbara Lindsay. From her notes, she wrote the chapter on John Fairfield as it appears in the book. It is by her own wish that her name does not appear on the title page. In that chapter, the opening scenes are fictional, based on Fairfield's known methods of work; "Judge Nelson," "Marsh," "Peter Wells" and "Virginia Johnson" are fictitious.

# Contents

# they
# took their
# Stand

# Freedom
# 1 papers

A newspaper man, P. D. East, had for several years published a typical small-town weekly journal, the *Petal Papers*. It was supported in the usual way by subscribers and paid advertisements by the comfortable, white merchants of Hattiesburg, Mississippi. Following the Southern custom, the interests of the Negro citizens of the town were ignored. Their names appeared in *Petal Papers* only if they "got in trouble with the law."

In 1955 East stopped writing news slanted solely to the "Southern way of life." The decision of the Supreme Court of the United States ordering an end to segregated public schools was scarcely a year old. The words of Chief Justice Earl Warren, the concurring opinion of Associate Justice Hugo Black of Alabama had been a cleansing wind blowing away the fog of silence in many places. Without pressing the point, East began to write about the concerns of *all* the inhabitants of Hattiesburg, black as well as white. He began to speak of justice. He wrote that in trying to limit the rights of Negro citizens, whites were endangering their own freedom. He wrote, "Before we can have justice, we must have truth." And he promised to print the truth.

Subscriptions were cancelled. Businessmen removed their advertisements from the *Petal Papers*. The Negroes in Hattiesburg were too poor to come to the paper's support.

The Easts' telephone jingled with hate calls night after night. His wife and little daughter were harassed by strangers and ignored by former friends. Through it all for six years, P. D. East wrote the truth about his Southern homeplace with gentleness and humor. For five of those six years virtually no Mississippi white man dared read the *Petal Papers*. Debts mounted. Finally East was forced to cease publication and move away.

Was it worth it, telling the truth? East could answer as did a former slave in the first years after emancipation a hundred years ago. "In slavery, you eats regular. In freedom you sometime goes hungry, but I choose freedom."

In the small town of Mansfield, Texas, on an October day, 1959, a tall, broad-shouldered, youngish man swung down the front walk of his home. Before he came to the end of the short walk, he set down the suitcase and the duffel bag he was carrying and turned back to give his five-year-old daughter and the two younger boys an extra hug. When he straightened up to his full height his eyes caught the eyes of his wife. Sadly, she knew and he knew that this leave-taking was not like others.

The family of John Howard Griffin, novelist and musician, was accustomed to his frequent absences for research or lecture tours. When he disappeared down the tree-shaded street this time, it was to enter into another world. If his children— even his wife—chanced to cross his path, they would not recognize him. Griffin, a white Southerner, was about to undergo a series of medical treatments that would temporarily change his fair skin to dark brown. Dark glasses, continually worn, would hide blue eyes; hair clipped close to the scalp would complete the transformation.

How else, except by becoming a Negro, Griffin had asked himself, could a white man expect to learn the truth of the black man's condition in the Deep South? He had to see for himself what it was like to become John Howard Griffin, no longer white but Negro, in a land where Negro and white Americans live side by side, separate—and never equal.

The movement of the black people to liberate themselves from second-class citizenship was nearing one of its intermittent peaks. Griffin's experiment was to last only a month. When the dye that changed his skin color wore off, he would return to the white world. In this respect he knew that this attempt to understand what it was like to be an American and black was not wholly valid. For the Negro there was no such easy retreat. But facts, set down daily in his journal and later published for the world to read, could speak for themselves.

John Howard Griffin, popular author, a leading citizen in his hometown in Texas, and John Griffin, Negro in Alabama, Mississippi, Louisiana and Georgia, trudging the streets looking for a place to eat and rest, a black man, jobless, ignored—they would be the same man, except for skin color. Did he guess, as he picked up his luggage and started off again, that he would emerge from the experience neither a white man nor a Negro but a human being—and free? But not quite free —for even as he walked toward the bus, John Howard Griffin was aware that no one is free until all are free.

The year 1963 was election year for state officials in Mississippi. In July eighty thousand Negroes cast their votes for Edwin King, a white Mississippian, the candidate of the Freedom party running for lieutenant-governor with Aaron Henry, a Negro, for governor. Their votes were uncounted, it is true. The vast majority of Negro citizens in the Southern states in 1963 were still denied the right to register to vote.

With the "freedom vote" for Aaron and King, in a mock election, history took a new turn. By standing for election, they had demonstrated that Negroes would vote if they were free to do so. The few who had managed to register were able to write in the names of their chosen candidates in the regular election in November.

For his stand by the side of the Negro Americans, Edwin King, chaplain of Tougaloo College was reviled, jailed on trumped up charges, ostracized in the state of his birth. Only the fact that Tougaloo was a privately endowed college for Negroes saved him from being deprived of his livelihood.

Why was he willing to take such a bitter risk? "Because," the young candidate for lieutenant-governor said, "white people in Mississippi are not free. We are prisoners of fear . . . our teachers are afraid to speak, our Christian ministers and laymen fear to talk to each other. The 'freedom vote' program means freedom for white and Negro Mississippians to solve their joint problems."

In the era when chattel slavery existed in the Southern states a manumitted slave, one who had purchased his freedom or had by other means been released from bondage, was given a "freedom paper" to carry on his person as legal proof that he was no longer a slave. East and Griffin and Edwin King carry no freedom papers. Yet, at a price, they have bought their freedom from the bondage of bigotry and racism.

According to Ulrich Phillips, speaking before the American Historical Association in 1928, "the central theme of Southern history is a resolve indomitably maintained that it [the South] shall be and shall remain a white man's country." It would be fairer to say that the central theme is and always has been a struggle *against* this concept of white supremacy on the part of Southerners who are not white! Yet the struggle has never been entirely between two ethnic groups living side by side for more than two centuries. In every generation the black people have had as allies white men and women to whom justice is of greater moment than skin color.

In the Declaration of Independence in 1776, a slaveholding Virginian, Thomas Jefferson, put into words the basic concept under which Americans in every generation have fought for freedom.

Through his long life Jefferson attempted to bring an end to the cruel paradox of a system of slavery existing in a nation founded on the promise that all men were "endowed with the unalienable rights of life, liberty and the pursuit of happiness." One by one he saw his proposals to abolish slavery defeated by compromise, by greed, by the poison of the myth of Negro inferiority.

The compromises began before the ink was dry on his first draft of the Declaration. The one small victory he was able

The Founding Fathers believed in liberty for all, an idea expressed in Samuel Jennings' *Genius of America Encouraging the Emancipation of the Blacks.*

to win thirty years later—the law abolishing the legal importation of kidnaped Africans into the United States—was nulli-
fied by widespread smuggling of slaves into Southern ports.
Even the solemn agreement that the vast Northwest Territory
should be forever free of slavery was ignored when the Territory of Missouri was, just five years before Jefferson's death,
admitted into the Union as a slave state. His own slaves
whom he freed at his death were not permitted by the laws of
Virginia to live as free men in the homes he left them. Three
times as many human beings were held in bondage in the
South when Jefferson died as had lived in all of America at
the time of the Revolution. And the truths he held to be self-
evident, that all men are created equal, equally endowed with
the right of life and liberty, had come to be called "glittering
generalities."

"I tremble for my country when I remember that God is
just," Thomas Jefferson of Virginia wrote, despairing. But
his idea of equality and freedom had been put into words
that were taken as a promise by the black slaves in the cotton
fields, by oppressed peoples overseas, even by a few, too few,
of his fellow white Southerners.

It was another Southerner, young John Laurens of South
Carolina who, when the Revolution was still in the making,
established for white youth the tradition of *acting* upon the
conviction that Thomas Jefferson's Declaration meant what
it said.

# John
# Laurens

Charleston, South Carolina, where John Laurens was born in 1754 was a small, beautiful city facing the sea. It was almost an island, with only a neck of swampy land between two rivers connecting its waterfront with the backwoods, an island that prided itself on its well-built houses, its lush, colorful gardens, its civilized, gracious living. Its spacious harbor, guarded by forts, was alive with the sails of trading ships. The wealth that created Charleston (named for an English king) came from the fertile swamplands, stretching inland from the banks of the two rivers, lands cleared, planted and harvested by slaves. The rice and indigo raised on the plantations made up the outgoing cargo. The goods brought into the Charleston harbor included tea from the East, fine cloth and ornaments, books, furniture, rare lilies, azaleas, olives, blossoming trees and even the very bricks the houses were built of. From England came clocks, harpsichords and a hundred other manufactured articles; from the Caribbean Islands, sugar, coffee and molasses, and from Africa, a constant stream of newly captured men and women to be sold into chattel slavery.

The slave ships carried only one cargo. Below decks they were crammed with human beings, chained, hopeless, stripped of all human dignity, envying their companions who had died at sea. Henry Laurens, John's father, for some years imported Negroes on his own ships. He gave up this enormously profitable enterprise for what he called "reasons of conscience."

There were many probable causes for the awakening of his conscience. The Laurens family were French Huguenots, forced to flee their own home in La Rochelle during the religious wars of the late seventeenth century. They had gone first to England and then had emigrated to the colonies, taking up residence first in New York with a large group of their compatriots, and then moving down the coast to South Carolina. John's grandfather, Jean Laurens, had earned his living and a respected position in Charleston as a carriage maker. A man of education, culture and humanitarian impulse, he was opposed to the system of chattel slavery.

So, in principle, was his son Henry. But when Henry married Eleanor Ball, the daughter of a landowner whose plantations were worked by slave labor, he was caught up in the general race for wealth. Insofar as the ownership of one human being by another can be mitigated by kindness, both he and his wife may be said to have acted well toward "their" Negroes. But the evils of the whole system enmeshed their lives, and by the time John was born (the fourth child, but the first to live beyond babyhood), Henry Laurens was in the business not only of using slave labor to work his own vast landholdings but of kidnaping, transporting and selling human beings.

The boat landing was within sight of the Laurens' garden-enclosed home. John, even as a small boy and companion of his father, could not help but see the wretched travelers as they disembarked and were herded into slavepens and prepared for auctioning. It was a sad business but very profitable.

Then, abruptly, Henry Laurens dropped the venture. What prompted his decision? Was it his own background and boyhood training? Or was it that he had to answer his own son's questions, had to watch the look of hurt bewilderment in the little boy's eyes?

Certainly the slave ships played a large part in John's deep and lifelong hatred of slavery. Before he was in his teens, two passions filled his mind—love for his country and a determination to rid it of slavery. The year was 1769 and the country he loved was not South Carolina alone but the whole narrow strip of colonies that some called *America*—an America identified in many minds with liberty.

John Laurens had, in fact, never been out of South Carolina. The various colonies were entirely separate from one another, and citizens of one colony were much more apt to travel to the mother country, England, than to visit another American colony. But as early as 1769 informal Committees of Correspondence had been formed and news was being exchanged between patriots in the North and South. The twin words *America* and *liberty* had been spoken together. The Committees' messengers had sped northward to New York and Massachusetts and had reached Virginia and the Carolinas in the South.

At sixteen John Laurens was an American in love with liberty. And he was clear, quite clear, in his mind as to the meaning of liberty. A letter written several years later to a fellow Carolinian gave his view.

> . . . I think that we Americans at least in the Southern colonies cannot contend with a *good grace* for liberty, until we shall have enfranchised our slaves. How can we . . . reconcile to our spirited assertions of the rights of mankind the galling abject slavery of our Negroes? I could talk much with you, my dear friend, upon this

subject, and I know your generous soul would despise
and sacrifice interest to establish the happiness of so large
a part of the inhabitants of our soil, if—as some pretend,
but I am persuaded more thro' interest than from conviction—the culture of the ground with us cannot be
carried on without African slaves. Let us fly it as a hate-
ful country and say *ubi libertas patria.*

*Where liberty is, there is my country!* And since the heart
and soul of the young South Carolinian belonged equally and
at once to America and to liberty, the dividing wall of slavery
must not be allowed to stand. For John Laurens, two sayings
were necessary: *Where liberty is, there is my country,* yes.
But also, *Where my country is, there liberty shall be.*

The letter was written from England two years before the
first antislavery society had been formed in America, and
John had been abroad for almost six years. When he was
sixteen his mother had died, and Henry Laurens had taken
him and his two younger brothers overseas to put them in
schools, as there were no proper schools in all of Carolina.

John had spent time in France and in Geneva, Switzerland,
and then returned to England to study law. Geneva was a
cradle of libertarian thought—the rights of man, justice, self-
government, government by contract, government without the
rule of kings. The ideas of the French philosophers Rousseau
and Voltaire; the writings of the Englishmen John Milton
and John Locke were under constant discussion—works that
were not entirely new to the young American. The books
were in his father's library, and the concepts were taking root
in American soil. But John Laurens remembered the slave
ships and the men and women and boys and girls in chains,
and he remembered that when he asked why, the answer had
been, "They have to be chained till they are prepared, till

they understand they are slaves." For John Laurens, the idea of self-government and the word *independence* that appeared more and more in letters from home meant just one thing: liberty throughout the land and for *all* inhabitants.

John's father was at the heart of the growing movement for independence, first as head of the South Carolina Council of Safety, then as president of the Provincial Congress of South Carolina, and as vice-president of the state when it ceased to consider itself a "province."

Finally in 1775 Henry Laurens traveled north to Philadelphia as a delegate to the Continental Congress. Plantation affairs "suffered extremely," Laurens wrote his eldest son, but he was not really troubled by this; his letters reflected the excitement of a man who knew that he was making history.

In answer, John wrote letter after letter, passionately pleading for permission to come home to fight for the country that was coming into being. In 1774 and 1775 the hopes for liberty were rising and the need to be a part of the struggle, his own struggle in every sense, overrode every facet of John's life—his studies, the responsibility to his family, even his love for the bride he had secretly married—Patty Manning, the seventeen-year-old daughter of a family friend.

But Henry Laurens insisted that his son finish his training. "Do not neglect," he wrote, "the proper means which lie before you for serving your Country—or rather for qualifying yourself *in due time* to serve it."

Due time! When people were fighting and dying for *his* dream? When the words in the heavy volumes of law all ran together to read, *Where liberty is, there is my country?*

"I long to be at home to share the fate, whether good or bad, of my countrymen," he wrote.

Emancipation of the slaves filled John's letters to his father, and Henry Laurens answered with sympathy.

> You know My Dear Son [he wrote], I abhor Slavery.
> I was born in a Country in which Slavery had been
> established by British Parliament and the Laws of the
> Country Ages before my existence—the day I hope is
> approaching when from Principles of gratitude and
> Justice, every Man will strive to be foremost in com-
> plying with the Golden Rule.

Then, unconsciously demonstrating the conflict in his own
attitude the letter continues without a pause:

> 20,000 Sterling would my Negroes produce if sold at
> Auction tomorrow—I am not the man who enslaved
> them; they are indebted to Englishmen for that favor,
> nevertheless I am devising means for manumitting many
> of them and cutting off the Entail of Slavery. Great
> Powers oppose me, the Laws and Customs of my Coun-
> try, my own and the Avarice of my Countrymen . . .
> What will my children say if I deprive them of so much
> Estate?

Still Henry Laurens saw what many a slaveholder failed to
see: the recognition of his "own Avarice," which held him
back from action. Henry Laurens concluded that these difficulties were "not insuperable," and asked for his son's advice
in the matter.

John's answer survives in the *South Carolina Historical
Magazine:*

> The equitable conduct which you have resolved upon
> with respect to your Negroes will undoubtedly meet
> with great opposition from interested men. I have often
> conversed upon the subject, and I have scarcely ever

met with a native of the Southern provinces or the W. Indies who did not obstinately recur to the most absurd arguments in support of slavery; but it was easy to perceive that they considered only their own advantage arising from the fact, and embarrassing themselves very little about the right. Indeed, when driven from everything else, they generally exclaimed: Without slaves how is it possible for us to be rich?

While this letter was on its slow way back to America, another young Southerner was composing the list of grievances against the English King that would be set forth as reasons strong enough to convince the world that the colonies on the shores of the Atlantic Ocean were justified in demanding independence from the mother country.

Thomas Jefferson of Virginia, thirty-two years of age, had walked the streets of Philadelphia all night long with only the stars and his racing thoughts for company while he searched for the right words to make clear the basic principles of freedom as an unalienable right. Now in the early hours of the hot July morning the draft of the Preamble was as good as he could make it, and with greater ease he was setting forth the acts that outraged the colonists. The climax of the long list was written without pause, without hesitation:

He has waged cruel war against human nature itself, violating its most sacred rights of life and liberty in the persons of a distant people who never offended him, captivating and carrying them into slavery in another hemisphere, or to incur miserable death in their transportation thither. This piratical warfare, the opprobrium of *infidel* powers, is the warfare of this *Christian* king of Great Britain determined to keep open a market where MEN should be bought and sold.

The draft was completed. It was ready to show to the other two members of the committee, John Adams of Massachusetts and the old and revered Pennsylvania philosopher, Benjamin Franklin, and finally to be presented to the whole Congress for approval.

On July 4, 1776, the Declaration of Independence was signed. Six weeks later John Laurens was directed by his father to hasten to France to confer with Benjamin Franklin on the means of getting aid for the colonies in their struggle for independence, and then to come home. John had heard news of the Declaration in England; in France, with Ben Franklin, he almost certainly held a copy in his hand.

He looked in vain for any mention of the enslavement of Africans brought to America in English ships by an English king. This was surely the greatest sin of King George against life and liberty!

It is not hard to imagine the twenty-two-year-old patriot striding about Franklin's room in Paris, the paper clutched in his hand, his neckerchief askew, trying to maintain a respectful manner as he stormed at his wise old host of seventy-odd years. *If they mean "all men are created equal," how can they do this thing? Will they let their private interest destroy liberty herself? Either ALL the inhabitants of our country are endowed with life and liberty and the pursuit of happiness or we destroy the concept before we have won independence at all!*

"The end of slavery is implied by the Declaration," old Ben Franklin explained patiently, earnestly.

Suavely he confessed that a clause condemning slavery had been removed from Mr. Jefferson's draft of the Declaration in deference to the interests of the Georgia and South Carolina delegations—and indeed at the desire of some of the New England shipbuilders as well. "Once they have subscribed to the premise of liberty we can rest assured that manumission will someday, somehow come about."

"Someday! Somehow! If we do not provide for freedom and enfranchisement of all our inhabitants *now,* when the words of liberty are on every tongue, we shall prove ourselves the hypocrites and liars that some Londoners now call us. Do you know what they are saying? 'How is it that we hear the loudest yelps for liberty among those that are drivers of Negroes?' Sir, we *must* act for freedom and enfranchisement or our beloved country will be torn with bloodshed and convulsions beyond our imaginings!"

"And shall we then disband the Congress and rescind the Declaration? Is that the word you wish to take to your father?"

John Laurens shook his head miserably. *Where liberty is, there is my country. Where my country is, there liberty shall be.*

"Let the Londoners talk," the old philosopher went on in his kindly manner. "We knew, John Adams and I, that the Southern brethren would never suffer this clause to pass in Congress. But look again at the Preamble, the Preamble which *all* agreed upon. There the abolition of slavery is inherent, is it not? What a happy talent for compromise young Jefferson has! Without the compromise, all would have been lost."

*And with the compromise, "only" the lives and hopes of 20 per cent of the American population.* Means would have to be found to make the two dreams—liberty and America—into one reality. John Laurens' lively mind went to work even as he turned back to the brief Preamble, those three hundred words that were to be of the highest consequence in the whole democratic struggle of mankind.

"The Declaration represents the cause of the whole of humanity," said Frenchmen of John's own generation, Frenchmen who included among their numbers the Marquis de Lafayette. Laurens met the young nobleman during his visit to Paris.

Lafayette, too, was preparing to sail across the ocean to enlist in the American army. Like Laurens, he was leaving a bride and comfort and safety in order to fight for his ideal of freedom. And the eyes of both young men glowed with the same vision in response to the promise of the Declaration and the glory of being in at the beginning of something new and great. *We hold these truths to be self-evident; that all men are created equal; that they are endowed by their Creator with certain unalienable Rights; that among these are Life, Liberty, and the pursuit of happiness . . .*

Yet there was a shadow, a question, a lingering concern in the mind of the South Carolinian that did not cloud the vision of the Frenchman. Lafayette did not share with John Laurens the sharp memory of slave ships at the wharf near his home, the sounds of weeping in the night from the slave pens where captives were prepared for auction. Nor had the young marquis heard educated and supposedly intelligent men offer absurd arguments in support of slavery—arguments that purported to prove Negroes a subhuman species, fitted by their very nature only for service in captivity. (That the proponents of the "inferior species" argument often found it necessary to spy upon their slaves in order to upset carefully laid plans for escape or insurrection was a bit of irony that John's observant mind could not overlook.) John understood only too well the real basis for the pro-slavery arguments. He had voiced in a letter to his father the fear that "the arts of luxury incidental to Riches and Commerce" had already crept in too far; that "the mercantile part" would hardly be persuaded to be "bereft of their accustomed profits."

But John did not share his premonition with his new friend. When Lafayette—three years younger than himself and a foreigner—repeated the noble phrases of the Declaration and spoke of the war in progress, he responded soberly, "I hope that we shall have patriots enough."

Lafayette made his way in disguise to Spain and sailed in his own vessel in the winter of 1776. Laurens crossed the ocean in an English ship. They both landed in South Carolina ports the following spring. The War for Independence was well in its second year. In the summer of '77, when Laurens joined Washington's army as an aide-de-camp, he found Lafayette already "a member of the General's family."

In the few weeks John had spent in Charleston, he had seen how little disposed his neighbors were to admit any inconsistency between their willingness to fight and die for liberty while they held their fellow human beings in perpetual bondage. Even his father, before leaving for Congress in Philadelphia, had insisted a little impatiently that discussions of this sort belonged to the future. True, Henry Laurens had made no objection when John proposed manumitting the personal slaves he had inherited from his mother. But giving Freedom Papers to a half dozen men and women and sending them on their way was not enough. *All men have unalienable rights to life, liberty, and the pursuit of happiness.* The promise of the Declaration was surely meant for Americans from Africa, too. Yet patriots of Charleston simply shut their eyes and ears to any argument that threatened their "property."

John Laurens realized that the gentlemen and ladies of South Carolina actually had come to believe in their own excuses for slavery. Ministers in their pulpits soothingly preached that Africans, being subhuman, had only one duty before God: obedience to their masters. And at their dinner tables the wealthy planters drank toasts to "George Washington and liberty" and secretly worried about the unrest among the Negroes, slave and free. They believed, of course, in the Declaration—but "all men" simply did not include chattel slaves. The few who, like Henry Laurens, now President of the Continental Congress, had some doubt about this state of affairs cautioned "silence" until the end of the war.

Early in September John reported for duty to General

Washington. At army headquarters, among the young officers clustered about the general, he met men as ardent as himself for liberty that should exclude no one because of the color of his skin. They included not Lafayette and his French friends alone, who had formed their judgments, as he had, abroad, but patriots from the New England states, from Pennsylvania and New Jersey. Five days after his arrival, when Washington gave battle to the British at Brandywine, Laurens fought alongside Negro soldiers from Massachusetts and Connecticut.

Washington, with ill-trained, ill-fed, ill-armed troops could do little more than harass the British as they invaded Philadelphia, and then retire to winter quarters at Valley Forge. In the terrible winter, when men drilled barefoot in the snow, almost starved, died of disease or exposure, John Laurens watched whites and blacks bear their hardships together, saw them buried in graves side by side. It occurred to him, with the shortage of fighting men, that there was a way to appeal to patriotic slaveholders to serve their own interests and at the same time to bring freedom to thousands of slaves in the Southern states where the vast majority were concentrated.

On January 14, 1778, at the height of that winter, he made the proposal to his father that "a well-chosen body of black men, properly officered, be trained in South Carolina to take part in the defense of the nation." They were, of course, to be given their freedom. That there would be obstacles to the experiment he was aware. Every Southern state and indeed the Continental Congress had passed laws forbidding the enlistment of Negroes. And even if such laws could be repealed, a few thousand in the army would not touch the heart of the problem. A few thousand? John proposed to his father that they begin with forty, chosen from the family plantations.

Head Quarters, 14th Jan., 1778

I barely hinted to you, my dearest father, my desire to augment the Continental forces from an untried source . . . I would solicit you to cede me a number of your able bodied men slaves, instead of leaving me a fortune.

I would bring about a two-fold good: first I would advance those who are unjustly deprived of the rights of mankind to a state which would be a proper gradation between abject slavery and perfect liberty, and besides I would reinforce the defenders of liberty with a number of gallant soldiers. Men, who have the habit of subordination almost indelibly impressed on them, would have one very essential qualification of soldiers. I am persuaded that if I could obtain authority for the purpose, I would have a corps of such men trained, uniformly clad, equip'd and ready in every respect to act at the opening of the next campaign. The ridicule that may be thrown upon the color, I despise, because I am sure of rendering essential service to my country.—

Your most affectionate<br>John Laurens

The father's answer brought forth potent objections, to which John replied:

The obstacles had presented themselves to me, but by no means appeared insurmountable. I was aware of having that monstrous popular prejudice, open-mouthed against me, of undertaking to transform beings almost irrational, into well disciplined soldiers, of being obliged to combat the arguments, and perhaps the intrigues, of interested persons. But zeal for the public service, and an ardent desire to assert the rights of humanity, de-

termine me to engage in this arduous business, with the sanction of your consent. My own perseverance aided by the countenance of a few virtuous men, will, I hope, enable me to accomplish it.

I confess, indeed, that the minds of this unhappy species must be debased by a servitude from which they can hope for no relief but death, and that every motive to action but fear must be nearly extinguished in them.

Henry Laurens had no faith in the plan, but he threw the burden of decision upon his son. Here spoke pity for the rich and not compassion for the enslaved.

Further doubts were expressed, further letters went back and forth between the son at Valley Forge and his father at York, Pennsylvania, where the Congress had taken refuge after the British captured Philadelphia. At last John put aside his dream. But ideas like this once launched in the world do not easily die. A year later, South Carolina was threatened by a British invasion from the army that had conquered Georgia. The governor came begging to Congress for troops. There were none to spare. It was Henry Laurens himself who brought forth his son's plan. A resolution was put through Congress with this amendment—that the masters were to be compensated for their "sacrifice" in freeing their "property."

Even so, John Laurens was overjoyed. He prepared at once to leave for Charleston, armed with the recommendation of the Congress. Had not Negroes fought at Lexington? At Bunker Hill? In the battles on Long Island?

In July 1779, John Laurens appeared before the Carolina Assembly. His proposal met with utter scorn. Not a single

Having seen whites and blacks fighting side by side in the War for Independence, Laurens proposed to free thousands of Southern slaves if they would take part in the defense of the nation.

member supported him. They said they would prefer to secede from the fight for independence before they would set up a battalion of blacks to defend the state.

Nevertheless they were so defended. Before the war was ended, one by one the states of Pennsylvania, New York, Delaware and all of New England freed slaves who wished to enlist in the militia. When Northern troops marched South, many Negroes were in the ranks. (From the first, numbers of free Negroes and freedmen had also served on the ships of the Navy.) It had become apparent that, where the system of slavery was not tied into the basic economy, the leavening effect of new world freedom was at work.

John Laurens made one more attempt. He asked his father to lease or give him one small plantation on which he would prove to the landowners that crops could be grown with free labor. No longer did he delude himself that merchants were the only ones who would consult their own interests above the interests of right and justice; but if they could have their profits and justice too . . .

Before any decision could be reached regarding this experiment, John and his distinguished father were sent abroad on separate missions for the Revolutionary government. Henry Laurens set out for the Netherlands. He was captured on the high seas and imprisoned in the Tower of London. John was commissioned to go to France to petition for money, guns and above all ships, to bring the urgency of their needs not only to the court at the Louvre but to Franklin himself, who after all could not know the despair and hardships of the four years of revolution.

Franklin was old and famous, twenty-six-year-old Laurens an unknown. But Laurens had lived through the disappointments and heartaches with Washington, he had fought on starvation diet, been wounded and a prisoner when Charleston fell into British hands. He knew that time was not on the side of freedom. With the determination and enthusiasm of youth he cut through court protocol and came away with some money, a few supplies and the possible promise of a fleet of ships.

Before he sailed for America again he had the pleasure of a few days with his wife, who crossed the channel secretly to see him and to plan their future when the war should end.

The end of the war! That was when the young South Carolinian's dream would be fulfilled: when "the trampled people tilling the land would prove how much they aspired to the rights of man, how capable of noble exertion for the public good."

He was with Washington in Virginia in October 1781 when the promised French fleet sailed into Chesapeake Bay and made possible the victory of Yorktown. The surrender of eight thousand British troops to the combined French and American army commanded by General Washington insured independence. However, John's sun-drenched home town was still in enemy hands. He rode south from the scene of victory to join guerrilla forces in the Carolina swamps.

On August 29, in a small, insignificant engagement at a fording place on the Combahee River, John Laurens was killed.

He was not the only patriot who saw that the Revolution could not "with good grace" be fought under the banner of freedom while a fifth of his countrymen remained in bondage, but he was one of the very few who lived in the Deep South and also owned slaves. And he was almost unique in his time in giving the emancipation of the American Negro the paramount place it deserves by those who talk of liberty. He was almost alone in his time in never thinking of oppressed slaves as a problem, a stumbling block, but always as *men* who had a right to fight alongside other American men for freedom.

# "F" is for
## 2 freedom

The war's end! One wonders what more John Laurens could have done if he had lived.

In 1783, when the treaty of peace was finally signed, one fifth of the new nation—600,000 of the 3,000,000 Americans—were of African descent. Of that number, the vast majority—about 550,000—were still, in a land dedicated to the proposition that all are equally entitled to liberty, held as chattel slaves. Of the remaining 50,000, more than half had been free before the Revolution was ended. In all of New England, slavery was abolished; in the Middle Atlantic states of New York, New Jersey, Pennsylvania and Delaware, laws looking toward abolition were before the legislatures. A few thousand slaves were given Freedom Papers in Virginia and North Carolina by individual masters, almost none in South Carolina or Georgia.

By 1826 when Thomas Jefferson died, the system of slavery was firmly established in America, grown twice its original size. There were fortunes to be made growing cotton in the unused rich soil of the newly formed states of Alabama, Arkansas and Mississippi. But cotton needed "hands" to plant and hoe and pick and bale. The law forbidding African slave trade was not allowed to stand in the way. Nine tenths of the cotton grown in the Deep South was tended by Negro slaves. Slave ships that had been rusting at anchor for a few years after 1808 shipped out again under Spanish or Portuguese flags. Thousands upon thousands of captive Africans were smuggled into Southern ports and marched inland by slave traders. In addition, superfluous slaves from the upper South were sold at great profit.

Not every white Southern family owned slaves—far from it. Two thirds of the white Americans in Virginia and the Carolinas never owned a single slave. Less than one fifth of the population owned as many as one hundred slaves; but wealth accumulated from slave labor gave this planter class enormous political and social power. They were the governors and the legislators and the judges.

The way for a poor man to get ahead was to buy a few slaves and take up land in the new states. For many, therefore, becoming a slaveholder was a goal that promised prestige and security.

Threats to the slave system came, not from Jefferson's law against importation, not from the majority of whites, but from the rising sentiment against slavery in the North and outside the borders of the United States and from the unrest among the slaves themselves.

Escape from plantations to the swamps or to Indian tribes or to the free states in the North; plots and insurrection (sometimes violent but never successful) gave notice that blacks were willing to risk death to win freedom. A few white Southerners were willing to help. The names of some of these men have come down in history, if only incidentally, when they were captured and executed along with accused Negroes. James Hall Mumford of Virginia, Joseph Wood of Louisiana are two examples.

George Boxley, himself a Virginia slaveholder, is more famous. He had tried to abolish the slave system by legislative methods; then in 1816 he armed his own and other slaves for rebellion. He was captured but escaped from prison, and has been termed a Southern-born John Brown. There were others who remain nameless . . . a North Carolina blacksmith who forged "weapons of freedom," and an old woman who stored food in her house by the side of the road where rebelling slaves planned to march.

The slaveholder's answer to these threats to their system came in brutal steps to fasten tighter the chains. Between the years 1820 and 1840 bodily punishments became more severe—beatings, iron collars, legchains were no longer rare. Armed patrols roamed the roads at night. Churches and Sunday schools where free Negro ministers from the towns might "infect" those from the plantation were closed. Manumissions were made very difficult or forbidden altogether. Free Americans of African descent were banished from most of the Southern states.

The greatest protection, however, the one thing that made the slaveholders feel most secure, was to keep the Afro-Americans forever in ignorance. Stringent laws were passed against teaching a slave to read or write. A white man or woman could be fined for teaching slaves. For the second offense they could be sent to prison. Literate Negroes were put under the lash for sharing their knowledge.

To read the Bible meant that a slave would learn of Moses and the escape of the Jews from Egypt, of the words of Jesus. Even more dangerous—they might read the first lines of the Declaration of Independence! Or a newspaper . . . To learn to write meant that a slave could forge a pass—not necessarily to escape, but merely to exercise a modicum of freedom of movement. To go to another plantation to visit a parent or child who had been sold away was frowned on. Knowledge was jealously guarded because knowledge itself is a mark of freedom. Yet there were slaves who learned to read and there were white Americans who risked prison to teach them.

# Sophia Auld

Hugh Auld and his wife, Sophia, lived in Baltimore, Maryland. Their box-like, small-windowed, frame cottage on Alliancia Street was near the Fell's Point shipyards. Alliancia was a typical city street, except that its uneven brick sidewalk ended rather abruptly at the busy waterfront. Instead of trees or a park, the edge of Chesapeake Bay sprouted a forest of masts and spars . . . Bardner's shipyard, Bearlane's shipyard and, between these impressive operations, Hugh Auld's own. The Auld shipyard was as small and insignificant as his house, but it was a beginning and he gloried in it. Through his back window Hugh could see across the broad bay to the green shores of the East Coast where his competitors had their country houses with lush fields and orchards tended by slaves. Their houses were imposing—slaves, homes, gardens, all coming out of the booming shipbuilding industry of which Hugh was a part.

True, he had only a precarious toe hold as yet, but he could already envision the moment when he would bring Sophia and his son to a porticoed summerhome set in wide lawns and weeping willows, with barns and slave quarters just over the rise. A stable full of horses and a pony cart for Tommy, and slaves to keep everything in order and call him "Marsa." And he would do it all himself . . . not as his older brother, Thomas, had done, by marrying into the slaveholding class.

Dashing and attractive, Thomas was married to Lucretia Anthony and comfortably settled in the Anthonys' long brick house on the river where the servants and field hands were *almost* his own. Hugh was welcomed there, too, often enough to get a taste of what it was to live in luxury, to have authority over dozens of blacks.

But Thomas was a member of the slaveholding community only by marriage. The man Hugh really admired was old Mr. Aaron Anthony. He had fought his way to wealth and power by his own efforts. This was the road Hugh had laid out for himself.

He only wished that Sophia had a little more ambition! To her, their social position—the shipyard that paid such meager profit, the little house where she had all the work to do—was a singing wonder. She had been a weaver when he first met her, supporting herself by her own industry. The work of caring for the four rooms, of tending their son was a joy to her. A perfect wife, except for her lack of ambition to rise in the world, or even to visit his brother's plantation—or what was practically his brother's.

"I'm a working girl," Sophia had said on their way home from the Christmas festivities the winter before. "I can't get used to hoop skirts and three silver forks at my place at dinner. Or to turning Tommy over to servants to be cared for, however kind they are to him."

She'd never known what it was to have a slave. It was time she got used to it, and Tommy, too. Since money was a little short and every spare dime he could earn had to go into tools and hired labor for the Yard, he was grateful—very grateful—

to the Anthonys for the offer that had come to him that morning.

"I'm loaning you a boy, eight years old, to be *Tommy's care-taker and companion,*" his brother had written. No bill of sale or gift went with the young Negro, Thomas Auld had cautioned. Fred (that was the slave's name) would still be the legal property of Aaron Anthony, as in fact the crew members of Tom's sloop were.

"But the old man won't last forever," the letter had said. "And I think you can consider the darky as Tommy's property. This, however," he had added, "is to be kept between you and me."

It was not unusual, Hugh knew, to make gifts of personal servants to children of slaveholding families when they were quite young. That way, the children grew up understanding how to exercise authority. Even though it might be years before Hugh's dream of the country house and a proper number of slaves came true, his son could begin right away—he would grow up a gentleman, a slaveholder!

The young shipbuilder exulted, walking home from church on that hot August Sunday. Hugh looked sideways at Sophia walking beside him. He couldn't make out what she thought about it. All she said, when she read the note from Thomas, was, "Only eight years old? Isn't that soon to take the boy from his mother?" As if the slave woman had maternal feelings like herself. . . .

Sophia probably was a little nervous. He'd have to give her time to get used to having a slave. She was so kind and gentle, he'd have to see that she didn't spoil the boy. As the preacher had said in his sermon, the white people of the South had a grave responsibility. *Let slaves be obedient to their masters.* Firmness of discipline from the beginning would pay dividends that Tommy would reap as his slave grew older.

"Where will he sleep? The boy, I mean." Sophia asked

abruptly. "Should we put another bed in Tommy's room?"

Hugh couldn't help but laugh at her anxiety. The house slaves, the young ones under foot in the Anthony kitchen, had no regular sleeping arrangements. If for any reason you went out to the cookhouse at night, you'd stumble on them huddled on crocus sacks or on the bare floor. In the city, in their little cottage, the kitchen was inside the house. Still, the boy could sleep there. Not in a bed, of course. But if in her goodness his wife wanted to rig up a straw pallet . . . And if he was going to be a companion to Tommy, he'd have to have something more than the customary tow shift to wear.

It was a relief to see, when the boy arrived that night, that he had been provided with a pair of linsey-woolsey trousers.

Freddie, as Tommy nicknamed his slave at once, was tall for his age, and quite intelligent-talking for a boy right out of the country. He didn't mumble but repeated almost correctly "Miss Sophia" when Hugh told him what to call his new mistress. He seemed to take to Tommy, following him to the back yard to see the child's new dog and then coming into the kitchen to stand respectfully in a corner, while Sophia bustled about, getting the evening meal.

There was one tense moment, when Sophia was dishing up the liver and grits. She had set Tommy's plate and her husband's on the table, then with a third dish in her hand looked hesitantly in the direction of the slave.

Hugh was across the kitchen in three strides. He pulled down a tin piepan, slapped grits and gravy onto it and thrust it out. With a nod of his head, he indicated that Fred was to take his meal outdoors. On the stoop, in the yard—anywhere out of sight. Not a word was spoken, but Sophia, red-faced, understood the rebuke.

Hugh made no complaint when she went to the barn later in the evening and came back with a feed sack neatly filled with straw, and he nodded approval when she spread the pallet and an old blanket on the kitchen floor for Fred to sleep on. The four inhabitants of the household said their evening prayers together.

After that first evening, Hugh left Fred almost exclusively to the care of his wife. He rarely saw the boy, and since Sophia never complained of his conduct, there was no need to exercise the authority of a master in the matter of chastisement.

The shipyard occupied most of Hugh's time. He presumed that Sophia kept Fred busy fetching wood, scrubbing, running errands and taking care of Tommy. At moments he thought with satisfaction of his new status as a slaveholder. It was a beginning, even though the slave was an eight-year-old child and only on loan, not purchased out of his own savings.

As for Sophia, she soon ceased to have any feeling of strangeness. Naturally gay and spontaneous, she enjoyed having two children instead of one. Under her kindness, Fred lost his shyness. "Miss Sophia" no longer had to say, "Hold your head up, child, and look at me when I'm talkin' to you." He answered smile for smile, gaiety with gaiety. She sang hymns while she worked, and when her husband was absent, read the Bible aloud with Tommy and Freddie as audience. Sometimes she would take Tommy on her lap to show him the pictures. With a casual gesture, she would draw the slave boy to her side.

When Tommy turned five, she bought a spelling book in a bright blue cover and said that it was high time to teach him to read.

"A is for apple, B is for boy." Swiftly she went down the alphabet which Tommy already knew. When she came to F, she smiled and said, "F is for Fred."

"And T for Tommy," her son chimed in, delighted.

The smile did it. The slave boy had retired across the room. Reading, he knew, was not for him. None of Master Anthony's slaves had been allowed so much as the touch of a book in their hands. He had heard, it is true, that his dead mother had learned reading. But she had been sold twelve miles away from the home place shortly after he was born. He only saw her a few times, secretly, late at night, before she died. And he wasn't sure she could read. He'd only heard it told. Nevertheless, the mysterious magic of the printed word set up a longing in his heart. Miss Sophia was his mistress now, and she had said F is for Fred and smiled across the room at him. He threw caution to the wind.

"Could I see the F? Could I look on? Could I learn to read with Tommy, Miss Sophia?"

"Can't you read, Fred? Didn't anybody teach you your letters?" He was such an intelligent boy his ignorance surprised her.

He knew the truth. He could have told her. He had been scarcely as old as Tommy, but he remembered when the name of Denmark Vesey and his insurrection way down the coast in Carolina was whispered in the quarters on the Anthony plantation, and in the big house, too. Denmark Vesey was a reading and writing man and he had gathered together a thousand slaves to fight for their freedom. The white people had caught him just in time—their time.

And they said, "That's what comes of reading." On the plantation reading, for blacks, was a sin punishable by flogging or worse.

Everything was different here in Baltimore. Maybe he ought to have told Miss Sophia. But the longing was too great. He moved up to her chair. Tommy was in her lap, and she reached the book in front of the child so Fred could share it. Gingerly he took the corner in one hand, *a book*. The first he had ever been allowed to touch.

"We'll begin over, shall we, Tommy?" Sophia Auld said. "A is for apple . . . that's the letter, pointed like a tent." Certainly, if Fred was to be a proper companion for Tommy, he should be able to read. And what a pleasure it was to see the look of delight on Fred's face!

The lessons went on every day for almost a month. Once he caught on to the trick of it, Fred was naturally quicker than five-year-old Tommy. He could read all his letters and words of one syllable without half trying. Three-letter words, that is. The next page of the speller was harder. When it came to five-letter words he still stumbled a little. One day he was doing so well that the reading lesson went on longer than usual. Or it may be that Hugh Auld came home early.

"Listen to Freddie, Hugh." Sophia was proud of her pupil's progress. "We've only been having the lessons a month! If he keeps up like this he'll be able to read the Bible for himself before the year is. . . ." Seeing the black look cross her husband's face, she faltered and fell silent.

Hugh Auld knocked the boy away with such violence that Tommy hid his face on his mother's shoulder.

"He wanted to learn." Sophia Auld caught her breath. "I thought—to read the Bible—to take care of Tommy right—I thought it my duty to teach him. Did I—was it wrong?"

"You are a fool," the man stormed. "Don't you know the harm reading can do? If you give them an inch, they'll take an ell. Learning will spoil the best black in the world."

"But how can it do harm to read God's word in the Bible?" For a brief moment, Sophia Auld stood her ground.

"Knowledge will forever unfit him to be a slave. A slave should know nothing but the will of his master. What will my brother say? You've done the boy no good but a great deal of harm. If you teach him to read, he'll want to know how to write. First thing you know, he'll write a pass that will get by the patrol and he'll run away. It's not safe, I tell you. I forbid you to let him set his hands on a book." Cold, harsh, his voice struck the gentle young woman like a hammer.

It was an order. Sophia Auld was inexperienced in the ways

of the slaveholding world but she was an obedient wife.

"I've been thoughtless, Hugh," she whispered in real humility. "I didn't mean to displease you. He's such a bright little boy and he and Tommy play so nicely together. I didn't think . . ."

Frightened into submission, Sophia Auld went no further with her teaching. She even bent over backward in keeping books and papers from the young slave's reach.

There were other whites, women and men too, who, though slaveholders, chose to ignore the dictates of law and custom. Bravely, defiantly, often secretly, they taught a few favored slaves in their possession to read and write. A dozen women whose names are forgotten were courageous enough to persist in their teaching even if they went to prison for it.

Unlike these, Sophia Auld kept her promise. But that month of teaching which she did so joyously out of kindness of one human being to another was historically important. Sophia Auld's sensitivity to human values was evident. Left to herself she exhibited no trace of the disease of white supremacy or prejudice. But the rules set by the few powerful slaveowners and the less powerful whites who, like her husband, longed to be part of the "in-group" were too strong for her.

The reason why this gentle young woman deserves a place in American history is somewhat ironic. The boy to whom Sophia Auld gave a start was known in later years to the whole world as Frederick Douglass.

F is for Frederick, for Fugitive, for Freedom. In 1838, when he was twenty-one years old, Frederick escaped from slavery. He had by then acquired a thorough knowledge of the Bible, of the writings of English philosophers, of the orations in *The Columbian Orator* (a volume he had bought with his first-earned half dollar). He had also acquired the skilled trade of a calker on boats and some deep scars on his back from the disciplinary lash of a slave breaker.

"Who would be free," he wrote years later, "themselves must strike the blow." His blows for abolition shook the whole system of slavery. In New England, in upper New York State, in the West and in England and Scotland his majestic wrath and keen wit were powerful weapons against slavery and prejudice. As orator, writer, publisher of his own newspaper, Hugh Auld's first slave became the recognized leader and spokesman for thousands, white and black. During the Civil War—which indeed through his influence as much as through any one man's became a war for emancipation—Douglass mobilized, at Lincoln's request, thousands of Negro troops, including his own two sons, to take up arms for the Union. After the war he pressed eloquently "to make this nation's practice accord with its Constitution and its righteous laws."

Sophia Auld's impulsive instruction in words of one syllable so simply begun, so harshly stopped, was the basis of Douglass'

Frederick Douglass was the boy to whom Sophia Auld gave a start; he became known throughout the world in later years.

education. Unwittingly she did more to end slavery than her outraged husband could have prophesied in his wildest fantasies. And her teaching had another unpredictable effect. For it is through Fred's writings that the Auld name is remembered. Douglass' healthy hatred of slavery was never wasted in blind rage against all whites, he never lost faith, never stopped believing "America could be . . ." This special strength was nourished by the thoughtless, reckless decency of a Southern white woman who reached out her hand saying, "Come, Fred, we'll start again at the beginning."

# 3 Charleston belle

The battle waged by Southern planters to preserve the system
of chattel slavery did not grow less fierce as the years went by.
Repressive Black Codes made the lot of the Negroes more
miserable but did not silence their pleas for freedom; com-
plaints to the Federal government of "malicious meddling from
the North" did not quiet the voices of outspoken abolitionists
such as William Lloyd Garrison and Wendell Phillips in
Boston or keep anti-slavery societies from springing up in New
York and Philadelphia and Ohio.

Apparently it was not enough to prevent slaves from learning to read. The immorality of slavery set forth in religious
tracts from the pens of Quakers, Methodists and Presbyterians
and Garrison's anti-slavery newspaper from New England, the
*Liberator,* were reaching people in the Southern states and
stirring up the never-quite-subdued sentiment for emancipation. Among slaveholders themselves were men who had never
ceased to deplore the system, who looked longingly, if somewhat vaguely, toward the day when their beautiful and much
loved Southland would be free of the shadow that hung over
it. Suddenly they began to speak out.

Measures taken in every Southern state were sufficient—or
almost sufficient—to keep abolitionist literature from the North
out of reach. In Maryland, for example, whites guilty of cir-
culating printed matter or pictures critical of slavery were given

prison sentences of as much as ten years. The penalty for free Negroes was thirty-nine lashes; for slaves, death. Abolitionist literature coming through the mails was publicly burned in front of the post office in Charleston, South Carolina. A post-master in Georgia was jailed for trying to protect a batch of anti-slavery tracts from confiscation. In New Orleans a large reward was offered for the capture of the editor of the *Liberator* "alive or dead."

However, in Tennessee, Southern-born Elihu Embree began printing the *Emancipator*. When Embree died, Benjamin Lundy, an itinerant printer, kept the paper going under the very shadow of slavery. Lundy, a Northerner, was finally forced to remove himself and his pernicious paper to Baltimore; but the stubborn North Carolina Quaker, William Swain, continued to put out his *Manumission Society* journal to the end of his life.

Farther west, in Huntsville, Alabama, the mayor of the town, a lawyer, James Gillespie Birney, wrote an article for the local paper, mildly critical of slavery, and favoring gradual emancipation and African recolonization. This was too much! Not even the prominence of his family—he was the son of one of the wealthiest slaveholders in Kentucky—could save him. Birney was ostracized; his law practice disappeared. Rather than give up his convictions, he chose self-exile.

James Gillespie Birney was neither the first nor the last of the exiles. The South permitted no criticism of slavery. Men and women spoke out not only at risk of reputation and liveli-hood, but at peril of their lives. One by one they were forced to leave. Rather than hold their tongues, ministers, slave-holders, students, Quakers who held no slaves exiled them-selves from the land of their birth. The list is long.

Those who had tried to silence them called them traitors. All, scarcely without exception, took their stand with the small band of abolitionists in the North. Few who left ever saw their homes again. Banished though they were, they felt themselves true Southerners, followers of the libertarian, democratic tradition set by Laurens and Thomas Jefferson.

# Angelina Grimké

Peggy, Angelina Grimké's personal maid, had lit the candles and turned down the bedcovers when the girl came home from the cotillion. Then the young slave had stood by as usual to remove her mistress' dress, brush her hair and perform any other service desired. But Angelina had dismissed her. Even though it was past midnight, she wanted to write in her journal. It was no trouble to call Peggy back, in any case. The girl slept on a pallet outside the door.

Angelina was in no mood for sleep. The cotillion—the first of the season—had been utterly boring, a tune played threadbare. She had gone only because her mother insisted. "You have to remember that you are a Grimké."

The Grimkés were not among the wealthiest families of Charleston, but Angelina's father, of French Huguenot descent and educated at Oxford, had been a Supreme Court judge of the state of South Carolina. Her mother was the sister of the governor of North Carolina.

The family position, church activities and overseeing her household slaves filled Mrs. Grimké's life. Angelina was the only daughter in the family of an age to attend social functions, now that Anna was married and Sarah had gone North to Philadelphia to pay her a visit. Eliza and Mary were just children. But Angelina, tall, graceful and lovely, was a satisfactory daughter in every way. Even without the Grimké name, her mother often said Angelina would have been a belle in Charleston society.

Obediently, Angelina had resigned herself to dancing polkas and the shottische. All evening she had responded with the usual answers to the usual gallantries of her dancing partners. She had listened politely to her mother's friends, seated on gilt chairs at the end of the ballroom, and had held her tongue while they complained about the laziness of their household servants or explained how right Mr. Calhoun was when he said in his latest speech in the Congress that slavery was the best thing that had happened for Africans in all their history.

Angelina Grimké had come home from the dance, sick with loneliness. Her journal was the only outlet she had for her true thoughts. She kept it locked away in a drawer and the key on a chain around her neck.

She bent over the page and wrote:

> October 10, 1845 . . . I pray the Lord that he make a way for me to escape from the land of slavery. Sometimes I think that the children of Israel could not have looked toward the land of Canaan with keener longing than I do to the North. . . .

Philadelphia? If only she could go there! Her brother might take her, if she asked him, when he went next month to see about selling the cotton crop. She could say that she was lonesome for Sarah. Henry wouldn't mind escorting her, with her maid, on a packet boat. Once in Philadelphia no one could keep her from setting Peggy free. She could do that by law. She had a right. Her father had given Peggy to her as a present on her tenth birthday. And Peggy had rights, too; a right not to be given away like a box of candy!

Angelina's blue eyes sparkled with excitement. All at once going North seemed not only possible but worthwhile. She wrote one more sentence hurriedly. *It's like a promised land, a pleasant land because it is a land of freedom.* Then she locked the book away.

The windows at the end of her room opened onto a small balcony. She stepped outside into the cool of the night. The decision to leave was so simple. Why hadn't she thought of it before? It wasn't just the thought of another winter of dances and concerts and hunt breakfasts, though that had helped. What made the difference was the newspaper Sarah had sent. It had come in last night's post, inside a French novel, *Marie,* by Gustave de Beaumont.

Fortunately she had opened the packet in her own room, because the newspaper fell out at once. Mr. Garrison's *Liberator!* Last year a bundle of *Liberators* had been burned in front of the post office. Henry had been there and described the whole thing at the supper table. Suppose he knew that his sister had a copy of the paper this minute under her pillow!

Angelina had written a letter to Mr. Garrison, praising his stand. Of course she couldn't send it. It would be stopped by the postmaster. She'd cried when she had to tear it up. But in Philadelphia . . .

Angelina leaned against the iron rail of the balcony and sniffed the night-blooming jasmine. There was a moon over the water. Palmettos and live oaks hid the shore from her sight, but the sound of the rippling waves was as clear as if she were standing on the quay.

Charleston was so beautiful. The whole Southland was, at

least such parts as she had seen. . . . The flat silvery sands, the cypress in the swamp, the sweet-smelling bay trees, the fields of rice along the Pee Dee and the Santee rivers. The cotton growing on the islands. The upland yellow pine woods, a little frightening, with gray trailing moss. The azaleas and sweet william. Sheer beauty—all of it. If only this blight were not on the land . . . the dark shadow of an enslaved people! To be free of it, to breathe a fresher air for a few weeks . . .

"I've made up my mind," she said, and turned back into the room. "Peggy!" She hardly had to raise her voice. The slave girl was a light sleeper. "You can help me get ready for bed now."

A pretty dress, she thought as she watched the gossamer blue dimity with puffed sleeves and high waist outlined with rosebuds being hung in the wardrobe. "I'll take it with me, North," she said to herself. And while her long hair was being brushed the prescribed hundred strokes, she toyed with the idea of sharing her secret with Peggy. But it wouldn't be safe to mention the word freedom. The girl might give the news away by a look, a gesture. Slaves were watched like hawks these days. Not until they were safely in Pennsylvania and Henry had left them would Angelina mention freedom papers.

"You look mighty pert this evenin', honey," Peggy said.

Angelina yawned to keep from answering.

Angelina Grimké arrived at her married sister's home in Philadelphia on October 20, 1835, a young lady coming on a visit with a trunkful of pretty clothes, her brother as escort and a slave girl her own age as her personal maid. This is the way many of the exiles left the South, unaware that like-minded people from all over the area were getting out. They were strangers still to each other, without a plan, knowing only that somehow they must be relieved of their self-imposed silence.

Often they came as Angelina Grimké did, just to get away, not as crusaders. Like Angelina, most of them had looked on the North "as a pleasant land of freedom." No floggings, no shots in the night by trigger-happy patrols, no auction blocks, no chained human beings tramping the roads. Nothing of this kind assaulted the eyes and ears of the newcomers. But neither was there in the North a ready welcome for their ideas. Abolitionists, North or South, were not popular. They were troublemakers who wanted to change a *system*. They were few in number, just beginning to come together in some sort of organized fashion.

William Lloyd Garrison, with his newspaper in Boston (fifteen hundred paid subscribers, mostly free Negroes); Theodore Weld, preaching and teaching and dodging irate mobs in crossroad settlements in Ohio and Illinois; Arthur and Lewis Tappan, highly successful merchants and inveterate reformers; these leaders together with a few Quakers, male and female, with their austere dress and quaint speech, two or three Negro orators such as Charles Remond and Henry Highland Garnet and a couple of British visitors had met to form an American Anti-Slavery Society. The first meeting had been held in Philadelphia but the headquarters were now in New York.

Theodore Weld was training lecturers as agents to go among the people to stir up sentiment for emancipation and the education of Negroes. The plan was publicized by Garrison's paper and financed largely by the profits from the Tappan store. The forces Weld was enlisting were drawn largely from Southern students, self-exiled.

Sarah had barely heard of the society when Angelina arrived. Nevertheless, she had read the *Liberator* whenever a copy came her way, and on some wayward impulse had sent the paper to Angelina in Charleston, little expecting the powerful effect it would have on both their lives.

Sarah met her younger sister at the door in the plain gray

dress of a Quaker, her dark hair concealed in a little white bonnet tied under her chin. Angelina was not surprised. Sarah had long ago left the Episcopal Church for the Methodist, and the Methodist for the Presbyterian. She was deeply religious and a seeker. This time Angelina was enchanted, because she knew that Quakers had been from the first against slavery and permitted no slaveholders to be members of the Society of Friends. She was all for joining at once.

But before she could become a Quaker, she had to arrange for Peggy's emancipation. Anna's husband, Mr. Lord, was able to help her with this. The Lords did nothing to encourage Angelina's decision, but they were not unsympathetic. If Angelina wanted to give a slave her freedom, it was entirely her own affair.

There were some tears on both sides when Angelina gave Peggy her freedom papers, but they were tears of happiness. Peggy was going to stay right in Philadelphia where there was a school to teach reading and writing, a school for Negroes, run by Negroes, many of whom had lived in the city for generations. She promised to keep in touch with her former mistress.

No longer a slaveholder, Angelina was prepared to become a Quaker. No more dancing, no more gossamer ball gowns imported from France, no jewelry. It was small sacrifice for the peace of mind she felt in the silence of the little meetinghouse. But she never managed the "thee's" and "thou's" in her everyday speech and she resolutely wore her own brimmed bonnet in place of the Quaker cap. It was warmer, she declared, and kept off the wind. Divested of its red silk, nodding rose, Sarah agreed that it looked sufficiently sedate.

The first copy of the *Liberator* that came to her hands in Philadelphia brought terrifying news. Mr. Garrison had been attacked by a mob and dragged through the Boston streets, tied with a rope like a wild beast.

"How can people in the North be for slavery!" Angelina cried.

"They're not exactly pro-slavery," Sarah, with greater understanding, explained. "The people up here buy cotton for their mills from the South. And sugar and tobacco, too. They don't want to upset anybody or lose their jobs. Mr. Garrison frightens people . . . and the bankers and men of property don't want to lose the money they've invested. Thee knows how it is."

Angelina knew. Nevertheless she sat down and wrote a letter to the editor of the *Liberator,* saying how sorry she was for his trouble, how much she admired him, how he spoke, without perhaps realizing it, for the silent people in the South who knew how wicked slavery was. She took the letter to the post office without showing it to anyone and mailed it to Boston with a feeling of elation. A letter wasn't much, but to one who had been forced to keep all her feelings pent up inside, writing it gave her a good feeling.

The next week, Angelina Grimké's letter was printed in the *Liberator.* In spite of the fact that the authorities in Charleston made such a fuss about not letting people read the abolitionist paper, the letter with her signature was reprinted in the Charleston *Herald.*

A few days later word came from Henry. The whole city was in an uproar. Their mother was prostrate with chagrin. "How could a daughter of hers . . ." and so forth. Angelina and Sarah had better return at once—no, on second thought they had better not. No one who was anyone would receive them. Ostracism would be the least punishment they could expect. If they had not been helpless females, they would be tarred and feathered.

Angelina received Charleston's excommunication serenely. She was, in fact, delighted to see her words in their hometown paper!

Sarah was inspired to write a letter of her own, and address it to the "Christian Clergy of the South." Angelina began another letter addressed to the "Women of the South." The wife of a slaveholder, she reasoned, suffered from the system almost as much as the slaves themselves.

She began her "Epistle" by showing how the condition of the slave in the Southern states differed from slavery as it is pictured in the Old Testament.

"Our form of slavery," she wrote, "is hereditary and perpetual." Slaves could be sold or leased. Slave families could be separated. They could not legally marry. They could not, under the present laws, ever buy their own freedom.

They were kept in ignorance. "Actually," she said, "the South denies that Negroes are human beings."

Even those who defended the system of slavery most vehemently had stopped short of extolling slave traders. But Angelina Grimké saw no difference in principle between the seller and the buyer. "If slaves were not wanted by the respectable, the wealthy and the religious in a community, there would be no slaves in that community and of course no slave dealers."

All the pent-up ideas Angelina had permitted herself to write in her secret journal were set forth in this letter to Southern women.

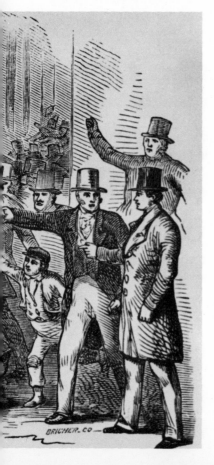

In Boston, Angelina read, Garrison had been attacked by a mob.

"It is manifest to any reflecting mind," she concluded, "that slavery must be abolished. The era in which we live and the light which is being shed on the whole world on this subject clearly show that the time cannot be far distant when it will be done. Now, there are only two ways by which emancipation can be effected—by moral power or physical force. It is for you to choose which of these you prefer."

Angelina and her sister were putting the finishing touches on their documents when a visitor announced himself at the home of Mr. and Mrs. Lord. A tall, beak-nosed man, middle-aged, wearing spectacles and already bald, the visitor's appearance was not impressive to one accustomed to the grace and vigor of Charleston aristocrats. But his name, William Lloyd Garrison, was magic!

Before he could mention the occasion of his call, Angelina pressed the letters on him. Would letters of this sort be useful? How could they reach the public?

He saw at once the special appeal the messages would have coming from Southern women.

"These should go out as pamphlets rather than mere letters," he decided, and asked permission to let them be printed by the American Anti-Slavery Society. Getting the tracts in print was only one more reason why the Misses Grimké must come to New York! Theodore Weld was giving a training course to agents about to go into the field. Angelina and her sister were invited to attend. There were of course no *female* agents, but a select number of ladies would be present, and it was hoped that a female society might be formed.

It was arranged that Mr. Garrison would escort the sisters in the railway cars next day. In New York they were the guests of a Quaker family and were introduced at once into Theodore Weld's training course. They sat shyly in the rear of the distinguished audience, a little overcome by the eloquence and knowledge of the huge, bear-like teacher. They listened with amazement to a lecture by Henry Highland Garnet, a Negro, an ex-slave. And as she listened it seemed to Angelina "that God intended her to do some great work."

At the end of the fourth lecture in the training course, Weld came to the sisters and made a surprising request: Would they like to become agents of the society to speak before women in churches, homes or even in the open air— wherever they could get an audience? Weld explained that the possibility of female agents had never really been considered before, but he had read their epistles and had always believed that women had a right to use their talents. As Quakers, the Charleston ladies had the sanction of their religion to speak. The pay, he explained, would be eight dollars a week.

Angelina's eyes danced. Sarah was grave, chin lifted and determined. At a nod from her older sister, Angelina answered demurely that it would not be necessary to consider payment. They had a small inheritance from their father. The help they would need was not financial but in the form of advice and further instruction. She drew a deep breath. "When could we start?"

Meanwhile, the society was having the pamphlets printed, with the names of the authors boldly on the title page. When completed they were distributed over the country, and copies sent into the South.

The pamphlets were publicly burned by postmasters in South Carolina and Georgia and Alabama. The Charleston authorities instructed the police that if Angelina Grimké should attempt to return to the city of her birth she should be held on the steamer while it was in port and must not be allowed to communicate by letter or otherwise with any person in the city. She was also threatened with mob violence should she visit her home.

The threats only served to make her an interesting figure to the abolitionists. She and Sarah began to address ladies' missionary societies in the small communities around the city, escorted always by one of the young men from Weld's training class.

Occasionally Theodore Weld was their escort, and Angelina confessed to her sister that she found him strangely attractive. But he seemed to avoid her if possible—a new experience for a Charleston belle!

From New York, Angelina and Sarah went on to Boston. Women attended their lectures in great numbers, and after a while men attended, too. It was unheard of for a woman to speak from a platform before a mixed audience, but the message seemed to Angelina too important to be stopped by criticism. The sisters resolutely continued their lectures through the winter and into the spring.

As their right to speak was challenged, Angelina was drawn into a defense of women's rights. Freedom for the enslaved and freedom for women to use the powers they were given by nature did not seem inconsistent to her. Weld worried lest her concern for her rights as a woman might weaken her influence as spokesman for abolition. He need not have worried. It was Angelina's broad and passionate view of human rights that made her so effective. *We hold these truths to be self-evident; that MAN is endowed with certain unalienable rights, among these, life, liberty and the pursuit of happiness.* The words were as true for the female sex as for the enslaved African!

In spite of Weld's worry and Garrison's distrust of political action, the Grimké sisters agreed to testify before a committee of the Massachusetts Legislature which was considering a petition for the suppression of the slave trade in the District of Columbia.

The strain and responsibility of so unfeminine an undertaking made Sarah take to her bed. Angelina in her demure gray dress and not so demure bonnet stood up to questioning of the legislators alone for three days. Opposition melted. The beautiful young woman was listened to with respect, both because she was a Southern aristocrat who had grown up in a slaveholding household, and because, under the tutelage of Theodore Weld, she had become one of the most eloquent of all the lecturers upon the subject of abolition.

"It is right for you to concern yourselves with the plight of the Negro," she told the gentlemen of the committee in her soft Southern accent, "because slavery is a *national* sin. Man has an inalienable right to liberty, and any denial of that right is an outrage against justice and decency. The sale of human beings as chattel infringes upon the prerogative of God; the auction block in the capital of the nation is an unpardonable denial of the principles upon which our country is founded."

The room in which the meetings were held was crowded. Each day when it was over, people pressed forward to shake Angelina's hand. She peered at the faces, dark and light, and smiled politely, wishing Theodore Weld could have been there, but relieved that he had not come until the hearings were over. But tomorrow—or the next day—

She opened her reticule, ostensibly to get out a handkerchief but actually to touch the folded letter which had all week been her talisman. A love letter—from Theodore.

Ever since their first meeting in New York, two years ago, she had been hopelessly in love with him, but of all the young men in the movement he was the least attentive. In the exchange of letters about her work as agent for the society, he had scolded as often as he had praised her. Especially had he seemed harsh in criticizing her "unwomanly" decision to speak before the committee. As if she courted the notoriety that seemed to follow her every act for the cause! Then out of the blue had come The Letter. It was marked "Personal," and she had opened it reluctantly, expecting another scolding. Instead, a letter of love.

There was every obstacle against their marriage, he had written. The difference in background; in religion (as a Quaker how could she marry outside the Society of Friends?); the vow he had made to himself not to marry while the millions of Americans languished in chains—everything stood between them, except his great love for her. In short, would Angelina consent to become his wife?

Angelina would. But she begged him not to come to see her to plan the wedding until after the legislative hearings. Even in their happiness, work came first. This Theodore understood. He had not even written during this trying week, but two days later he was on the doorstep of the home in Brighton where the sisters were staying, and two months afterward they were married.

The wedding of Angelina Grimké and Theodore Weld, at the Lord home in Philadelphia, marks a high point in the history of the part Southern exiles played in the abolition movement. The date itself was determined in regard to events in the movement. The wedding took place one day after the close of the 1838 convention of the Anti-Slavery Society, which Weld had to attend, two days before Angelina was to speak at the convention of the Female Anti-Slavery Society in Philadelphia at the newly built Pennsylvania Hall.

Forty guests were invited to the ceremony, more than half Southern "exiles" whom Weld had drawn into the movement. James Birney was present and Amos Dresser, who had been lately whipped in public in Nashville, Tennessee. The Allen brothers, forced to leave Alabama, had come with other Lane Seminary students from Ohio, and Augustus Wattles.

Several Negro friends were among the honored guests, two of whom, Peggy and another, were liberated slaves who had belonged to Angelina's father.

Angelina's dress was Quaker gray, though she knew she would be read out of the society for marrying a Presbyterian—as Sarah would, for attending the ceremony. The cloth for their dresses was woven from "free" cotton grown on a farm where there were no slaves. The wedding cake, too, was made of "free" sugar.

On the second day after the wedding, Angelina gave her speech in Pennsylvania Hall, built "as a temple of freedom." She learned how unpopular it was for a woman to address an audience on the subject of slavery. A mob surrounded the building and brickbats flew through the open windows, but she went on speaking for two hours, pausing only once to "thank the Lord that the apathy of the city has been disturbed by the force of truth."

The next night when Lucretia Mott addressed the convention, rioters burst open the doors of the beautiful hall and burned it to the ground. Theodore and Angelina comforted themselves that every new outrage brought new strength to their side. However, neither Angelina nor her sister ever spoke in public again.

For Sarah, who dreaded facing an audience, Theodore Weld's decision that the Grimké sisters should retire from platform appearances was sheer relief. For Angelina? A born orator, at the height of her powers? She never voiced a regret. It was enough to be the wife of Theodore Weld.

Though she ceased to speak, Angelina Weld by no means retired from the struggle. Two years later a monumental volume was printed showing conditions in the slave states.

*Slavery as It Is* was published anonymously, but everybody knew it was the work of Angelina and Theodore Weld. The document was devastating. Because the facts were from authentic Southern sources and were backed up with names, dates and places, the evidence could not be denied.

By 1861, when war came, the Grimké sisters were white-haired. Angelina was able only to watch and hope and suffer on the side lines. She gave of her strength to support the demand of Negro Americans to be enrolled in the Federal Army to fight for their own freedom. She raised funds to send nurses to the battle lines to tend the wounded, and teachers to the tent schools to teach the refugees from slavery, and grieved that she was not well enough to go herself.

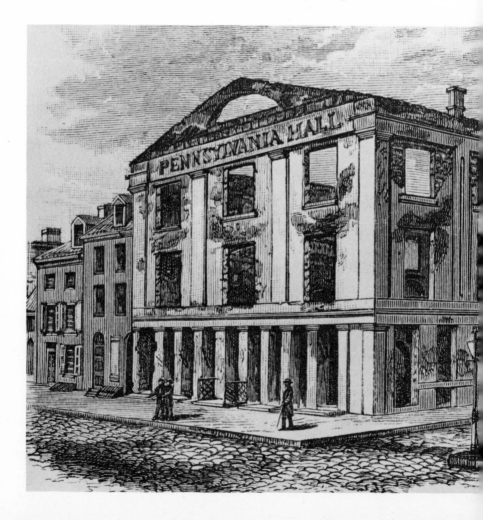

For years she had been cut off from her family. At the close of the war, however, letters came from Charleston. Mary and Eliza, the younger sisters, wrote that their mother and brother were dead, that the plantations lay idle since their slaves had been taken from them. For everything that had happened they blamed Angelina.

"They're not far wrong, my dear," Theodore said with a sad smile. "You Southerners, white and Negro, who left your homes and came away, brought truth with you, and the truth has made us free."

Burned by rioters, Pennsylvania Hall stood in ruins the day after Angelina Grimké spoke against slavery.

One more event brought comfort to Angelina's last years. She and her husband and Sarah were teaching in a small school near Boston when she learned that two Negro boys, Archibald and Francis Grimké, were at a school for freedmen in Pennsylvania. Grimké! Angelina made inquiries and found that the orphaned boys working their way through school by waiting on tables were the sons of her dead brother. Their mother was Nancy Weston, a slave in the Grimké household.

Since the beginning of slavery, women had borne their masters' children, officially unrecognized but a bitter fact of life, of common knowledge in the South.

What was done in the past could not be undone, but with staunch simplicity Theodore said, "Your brother's children belong with us, in our care."

Francis and Archibald Grimké came to Massachusetts that summer. The combination of shared background and shared concerns forged strong ties between the aging Angelina and her brother's boys. Negro and white, the members of the Grimké family were a close-knit unit.

Both men, after Angelina's death, had distinguished careers, and Archibald's daughter, Angelina Weld Grimké, became a well-known poet. The delicate lyrics of Angelina's namesake, which appear in many anthologies, are like an echo from the young abolitionist's journal, "the pleasant land of freedom" still coming into being.

# Railroad
# 4 man

Freedom is the moon and men the ocean tides, and the Negro American was determined to have his liberty. Because after 1850 every means to communicate that fundamental desire was shut off, the system of slavery in the South simply burst at the seams. This is the meaning of the Underground Railroad, of the great exodus of fugitives across wide rivers, over rugged mountains, hidden in the holds of ships, by any means or method under any risk—provided the journey ended in the North, envisioned as a land of freedom.

The great importance of the Underground Railroad was not that sixty or a hundred thousand former slaves escaped their bondage; it was that, by their escape, by their physical presence throughout the country, with the marks of the lash on their backs, the scars of irons still visible on their legs, by the dangers they had undergone to get away, the fugitives brought testimony that Negro Americans were determined to be free men.

It was these dark-skinned refugees, freeing themselves from slavery, who formed the barricade against the determination of the few to extend slavery over the whole of the land. It was these refugees around whom white Americans rallied to strike their blows against the slave system, and—in a few states above the Mason-Dixon line—to pass personal liberty laws in defiance of the Fugitive Slave Law.

# LIBERTY
## NEW ARRANGEMENT

The improved and splendid Locomotives, Clarkson and Lundy, with their trains fitted up in the best style of accommodation for passengers, will run their regular trips during the present season, between the borders of the Patriarchal Dominion and Libertyville, Upper Canada. Gentlemen and Ladies, who may wish to improve their health or circumstances, by a northern tour, are respectfully invited to give us their patronage.

SEATS FREE, *irrespective of color.*

Necessary Clothing furnished gratuitously to such as have *"fallen among thieves."*

lingo in advertising passage to freedom.

# LINE.

## --NIGHT AND DAY.

"Hide the outcasts—let the oppressed go free."—*Bible.*

☞For seats apply at any of the trap doors, or to
the conductor of the train.

**J. CROSS,** *Proprietor.*

N. B. For the special benefit of Pro-Slavery Police
officers, an extra heavy wagon for Texas. will be furnished, whenever it may be necessary, in which they
will be forwarded as dead freight, to the "Valley of Ras-
cals," always at the risk of the owners.

☞Extra Overcoats provided for such of them **as**
are afflicted with protracted *chilly-phobia.*

The language of the Underground Railroad was a symbol of the railroad-building times. Its "rolling stock," its "captains," its "stationmasters" and "conductors" were words used to indicate the escaping slave and those who helped him on the way.

The *fact* of the Underground Railroad was a symbol, too, and more than a symbol: It represented and gave a new life to faith in a nation based on every man's inalienable right to liberty. Nobody knows how many thousands of Americans, black and white, slave and free (in rare instances, even slaveholders) were involved in the Underground escapes during the 1850s and '60s. The names of some three thousand have been identified, most of them as stationmasters doing the work of raising funds and providing food and hiding places across the line. There were the steamboat captains who carried people across Chesapeake Bay or the Ohio or the Mississippi; hundreds who on trains or in wagons managed to get the fugitives from the free-state borders past the ubiquitous slave hunters to the Canadian border. There were also those others—far fewer in number—who went into the land of slavery as conductors. There was Harriet Tubman, the Moses of her people, who made nineteen trips after she escaped in 1849. There were Josiah Henson, Samuel Burris, Thomas Garrett, the Delaware Quaker, Calvin Fairbank of Kentucky. There was Levi Coffin who was known as the "president" of the Underground Railroad. He was also a Quaker who had left North Carolina in 1821 and settled in Cincinnati, Ohio, just across the river from slave territory.

The records give many hints of the involvement of other white Southerners, but for reasons of protection their names are almost never known. We hear of the son of a prominent slaveholder in New Bern, North Carolina; of members of "prominent families" in Alabama and South Carolina. We know that the hill folk of Tennessee and Virginia, along the

Appalachian range, were ready to pass along fugitives and turn back the posses of slave hunters. And we know that one of the bravest, most daring and dedicated of the conductors was a white Southerner and a member of a slaveholding family—the young Virginian, John Fairfield.

# John Fairfield

The room was not large, but it was high-ceilinged and imposing, almost oppressive with mahogany paneling and reddish-brown velvet draperies. It served both as library and office. At one end an immense flat-topped desk was buried under papers—letters, lists and ledgers, worn classics bound in leather that had spilled over from crowded shelves.

At the other end of the room, in front of an open fire, two men sat relaxed and comfortable, sipping an iced drink and conversing. The host, a planter and retired Chancery Court judge, lounged back in his brown leather chair, well satisfied with the business transaction just completed. He had been promised a fine price for the poultry that he was to deliver in Nashville. Besides, he found the company of the young agent of the produce firm, who had introduced himself as John Windsor, much to his liking. They talked the same language. The Virginian obviously came from a good family, seemed to have connections all the way from Roanoke to Richmond.

They talked about cousins and hunting dogs and the stream of movers on their way to the Far West, whether there really was gold in California and whether the Germans were going to ruin Texas with their "free-soil" agitation. They talked about the weather and how this year's tobacco worms looked bigger and fatter than ever, how expensive it was getting to keep a good growing stock of mules and horses—or for that matter, Negroes.

The talk drifted to politics and the new Fugitive Slave Law. "It ought to stop the abolitionist devils who were out to destroy the South," the planter said.

"Windsor" nodded in seeming agreement. "At least it will cut down the slave stealing . . . that is, if the Federal marshals are dependable—"

The planter frowned. "Dependable! You can't depend on anybody." The older man had risen and was pacing the floor, twisting a gray forelock and evidently winding up for a long tirade.

"Did you read what Justice Green came out with in Memphis? 'A slave is not a horse. He has mental capacities and an immortal nature that constitute him an equal with his owner.' Equal, Windsor—a state judge coming out with crazy ideas like that! Sure as I'm standing here, some uppity colored barber's going to go around repeating it. Next thing you know, one of your good, loyal hands that loves you, hasn't a worry in the world, singin' while he works—"

"Singing while he works—if you're watching him—" The purchasing agent chuckled soothingly and took a sip of his drink. "I really don't know, Judge, when I've enjoyed a toddy as much as this one."

The comfortable image of the "naturally lazy, contented" slave had already relaxed the slave owner's twisted forelock. When his toddy was praised, the host beamed and stepped to the door.

"Marsh! Marsh!—Where is that no-count—It's no wonder he forgets where he's goin'. I would, too, if I moved that slow."

"Yes, *sir*, Marsa." A stocky, dark-skinned man in white coat appeared.

"There you are! Sweeten Mr. Windsor's drink, Marsh. And get a couple of logs on the fire."

"Seems a likely fellow," Windsor commented, giving up his glass.

"Not bad, not bad. Got offered a thousand dollars for 'im the other day. But I wouldn't sell. Old Marsh wouldn't know what to do without me to look after him, would you, boy?"

"No, sir, sure wouldn't." The man looked up from the fireplace with a broad grin.

"Well, any time Judge Nelson gets tired of you, Marsh, he can let me know. I'm always on the lookout for fellows with some get-up-and-go. I reckon you'd like to do a little traveling."

"Well, now I'll tell you, sir," the slave answered amiably, "that travelin', it's all right for some. But old Marsh were raised on the place. Like old terrapin, have to carry my house on my back, do I go somewheres else."

"That's the truth." The master laughed. "Marsh took a notion to go over the Summer Ridge a couple of weeks ago. Wrote him out a pass. And do you know, he wasn't gone three hours. Gets out on the road, hears a screech owl and back he comes, chuggin' and puffin' like a steam engine on the Lookout grade!"

"Screech owl say go on home. 'Argue with owl at night,

somebody be dead befo' light,' " the Negro quoted, adding in a stage whisper, "Fact is, I just ain't got the travelin' kind of feet."

As Marsh high-stepped from the room, master, slave and visitor joined in hearty, intimate laughter. Or so it seemed to Judge Nelson.

"Let the fanatics at the North fuss and fume," he said expansively. "We understand our people, eh, Windsor?"

A week later the supposed egg produce agent dropped in to the Nelson plantation to say good-by. He found the planter pacing the floor, struggling with the wording of an advertisement for the runaway slave column. Marsh was gone! And that wasn't all. Three prime field hands had disappeared. And two females. Close to five thousand dollars' worth of property at today's market. And not one a habitual troublemaker. It had been a year since any of them had needed the lash.

When the paper with his ad came out the next week, Judge Nelson wondered if some meddler hadn't come sneaking through the valley. A total of nineteen slaves were advertised as missing from his and other plantations in the vicinity.

"Windsor" had been gone ten days when one last bit of pertinent information came into the judge's possession. He made the trip to Nashville with the wagon-load of poultry and found no such produce outfit as the one the Virginian had been representing. Discreet inquiries convinced him that, in fact, there wasn't any such person as John Windsor of Roanoke.

Tight-lipped, Nelson recalled the visits over a period of weeks, the friendly banter with Marsh that day, the hearty

Notices for missing slaves appeared in a Richmond newspaper.

# RUNAWAYS.

**TWENTY-FIVE DOLLARS RE-WARD.** — Runaway from my place, in Chesterfield county, Va., my Negro Man BEN JOHNSON, of black color, about 5 feet 10 inches high, weighs about 175 lbs., apparently 45 or 50 years old, and is a good cook, and is probably hiring himself to cook in Richmond or Petersburg. The above reward will be paid for his safe delivery to me at PULLIAM & Co.'s office, or safe lodgment in some jail. He came from Petersburg. Left home 1st March last.

ap 17—tf      ALBERT C. PULLIAM.

**$25 REWARD.** —Runaway, on the 29th of March, a woman named NANCY, whom I purchased of H. Stern, of this city. She is of medium size, rather spare made, of a ginger-bread color, has a diffident look when spoken to, is twenty-three years old, has a blister scar on her neck. She was sold last Christmas at the sale of Wm. Andrews, dec'd, nine miles above the city. She may now be in that neighborhood, or near Slash Cottage, as she has a mother living at Mr. Wm Winn's, near that place, in Hanover county. She was hired to Mr. Samuel Allen, of this city, last year, and has a husband hired to Mr. Ballard, at the Exchange Hotel, by the name of Dolphius. I will pay the above reward if delivered to me in Richmond.

ap 16—1w*      R. B. WOODWARD.

**$20 REWARD.** —Runaway from the subscriber, on the first day of this month, a NEGRO WOMAN named SARAH. She is about 40 years old. She is from the estate of Samuel Leake, and is now held by Walter D. Leake, Trustee. She is now in Richmond, with a forged pass. She has lived in Richmond for several years. She lived for the last two years with Mr. L. B. Conway, on 2d, between Broad and Marshall streets. She has two daughters; the oldest is an invalid, the other a sprightly girl, 11 years old. She has two sisters in Richmond, one living on Marshall, between 2nd and 1st streets, the other on St James street, near the corporation line. I will pay the above reward if sent to me at Ashland, or confined in jail, so I can get her again.

ap 4—1m*      HENRY SAUNDERS.

laughter—at his expense! He considered turning heaven and
earth to find the villain. But what if his business rivals
found out he'd been entertaining a slave stealer—an outlaw!
Or his political enemies? They'd make mincemeat of him.

Quietly the planter went home and removed from his
ledger all reference to the poultry transaction.

The woods smelled damp and fresh, and small showers of
rain water plopped down on horse and rider from the yellow
poplar trees and the pin oaks as John—recently "Windsor"—
Fairfield rode through a deep wooded area just over the
Kentucky border, going north from Tennessee. It was dark—
pitch-black, pre-dawn dark. Only a few late-blooming dog-
wood blossoms seemed to have shape or form. They marked
the course of the stream, like lamps reflecting their own
light from within. The creek itself, which would be nothing
but a trickle in the summer, was rushing along as if it had
an important engagement to keep. As important as his own.

An owl screeched and John pulled up on the reins. He
was drenched to the skin and shivering a bit, but thunderstorm or no thunderstorm, he hadn't time to look for shelter.
He waited for another moment, listening.

"No, go ahead, girl," he whispered to the mare. "That
owl has wings."

He wondered if he could have missed the turn in the
pouring rain, and dismissed the idea. That would have
meant missing the rendezvous with the eleven men who
had started north alone. And that just couldn't happen.

A few hundred feet more, and the sound of a waterfall
became distinct. The trail sloped sharply downward, then
disappeared entirely. With a sigh of relief, John dismounted
and tossed the reins lightly around an overgrown sassafras
shrub. The screech-owl sound came again. This time it was
followed by three quail calls. Quickly John unloaded the

saddlebags, untied the reins, turned the stolen mare about-face and started her home with a slap on the flank. "Home you go, my girl. You know you can't argue with the screech owl," he said cheerfully, knowing that this last "owl" made up in wit what he lacked in wings.

He moved cautiously down the slope, half carrying, half sliding the saddlebags and singing the *Drinking Gourd* song. *Follow the Drinking Gourd*—Drinking Gourd, Big Bear, Old Man's Wagon, the Dipper . . . so many names for the seven stars that pointed to the one star leading north—"For the old man is a-waiting for to carry you to freedom . . . follow the Drinking Gourd."

"Here, let me take those!"

John would have gone right by the cave entrance if Marsh hadn't stopped him. "Is everybody here? Everybody?" He was still a little nervous, worn down by the responsibility of having handled so large a group of fugitives at one time. Too many, even when divided as they were into two groups.

"All eleven of us, Mr. Fairfield," Marsh answered. "In the cave. It's a whoppin' big one, like it showed on the map you gave Pete. Did the others get off? Come get dry by the fire and have a dipper of coffee."

"They got off. And I made it here as fast as horses could bring me." John Fairfield entered the mouth of the cavern, new to him but not new for the Underground as a hide-out.

John Hatfield, the Negro stationmaster in Cincinnati, Ohio, had said that it had been used for five years—maybe for ten—as a rendezvous by the black conductors who'd been guiding fugitives through the slave states on this route to the Ohio River. (Dozens of the five hundred or more guides had spent days in this hide-out, some free men, some still slaves themselves in the area, willing to wait a little longer for freedom so they could send others from a distance on their way.)

John Fairfield was glad he had a safe place to send this body of strong young men to wait for him. As it turned out, Marsh and Peter Wells, a friend from a neighboring plantation, had collected twice as many people who wanted to make the trip as he had expected. He was a fool to have risked it, but so far it was working out fine. His only worry was the delay. They'd been held up too long.

In the final meeting in the woods, the night they had set out from Judge Nelson's plantation, John had divided the group of fugitives. First, he sent nine young men ahead to the cave with Marsh and Peter Wells. (Marsh was the reason he'd come to the area in the first place. He'd met Marsh's brother in the colony of escaped fugitives in Windsor, Canada, and had undertaken to bring Marsh out of slavery.)

When, as Judge Nelson's guest, John managed to make himself known to Marsh, the overjoyed slave had brought Peter Wells to their first meeting in the woods. In the following weeks those two had collected sixteen other people, some with money to pay their expenses, some without a cent. The eleven young men were no problem, but the others were too young or too old for the kind of trip Fairfield knew they would have through Kentucky. Still, they had waited a long time for a conductor. He hated to leave anybody behind. If it was in his power he would bring every slave in the South straight to the "lion's paw" of southern Canada.

By the Saturday night of the escape, every one of the young men had been provided with pistols or knives and had given his word to defend himself if attacked. Aside from the protection weapons gave, the fugitives needed to have the self-respect which, in the violent society of the times, came with carrying arms. With weapons and compasses and the map, the young men had set out alone to travel due north at night on foot to wait for Fairfield in the cave on the way to the Kentucky border.

John sent the second group, consisting of one old man, three women, two girls of twelve years or so and a frail sickly boy, eastward along the banks of the Cumberland River. Their orders were to get as far along as they could. He would pick them up with the wagon at daybreak.

The plan for those troublesome seven had been made some weeks ahead, while John was still posing as a poultry dealer. He gave out that he was going on a trip west to Memphis and would come back to close the deal with Judge Nelson. Instead he slipped into the next county and changed to his favorite role of tinsmith peddler. He bought a stock of goods and a wagon. He redesigned the wagon a bit to suit his needs and painted it a conspicuous red. He drove it around the countryside, not with a pair of horses, but with three—a bay, a gray and a sorrel.

Anybody in the foothills who saw the peddler driving by would be apt to remember the vehicle, which is just what he wanted them to do. He made a point of driving the roads in the early hours of the chilly spring mornings when the patrols were still about. Then he hid the wagon in an abandoned barn and was ready to become John Windsor of Virginia once again. Things had worked out smoothly at daybreak Sunday morning, all according to plan.

Sipping coffee in the cave four days later, John chortled as he relived the scene. "I dressed Miss Johnson—she's tall, you know, and fair-skinned—in my peddler's outfit," he said. "She had to cut off the braids she was so proud of, but it couldn't be helped. The children and the other two women lay flat in the wagon under the false bottom. There were cracks enough in the floor for them to breathe, and the trip with three good horses didn't take long to the next station in the underground."

The stationmaster there would pass them along straight up the spine of the Appalachians through Virginia and Maryland to Pennsylvania. The mountain route was the path where white hands as well as black were ready to help.

Peter Wells wanted to know what he'd done with the old man. "Turned him into a woman, I wouldn't wonder."

"Exactly that," Fairfield replied. "With a shawl over his head, a wide skirt and an apron, Preacher Jones was the picture of an old granny. A little on the brown side in the cheeks, but that could come from sunburn, traveling around the country in an open wagon. I busied myself with the pots and pans until Virginia Johnson nodded "Mornin' " to a couple of patrollers who were used to seeing me out early in the day. When they didn't look twice, I gave her instructions to the station, swung off the wagon at the next handy spot and 'borrowed' a horse out of a pasture."

"You'd better get some sleep, sun's coming." Marsh spread a blanket on the floor of the cave.

John Fairfield shook his head. This was his seventh trip as conductor on the Underground Railroad—he was used to going without sleep. The rest of the trip was going to be rough. Since the 1850 Fugitive Slave Law, kidnaping had become big business in Kentucky and on both sides of the Ohio River. These men might run into violence or even death before they got through Kentucky. But nothing, even getting killed, could be as bad as the slavery they were leaving behind. In slavery they had been killed a little bit every day of their lives.

The next hours in the cave were spent in rigorous training. At the end, they were not eleven fugitives and a Virginia gentleman who was leading them to a Promised Land; not eleven docile slaves ready to follow a conductor of the Underground; not a group of adventurers; but an army of twelve angry soldiers.

This had not always been John Fairfield's way. His first trip—three years before—had been made in the spirit of high

adventure, with nobody along except Bill, a slave and his childhood friend. Deep anger at the slaveholders, the oppressors,
had been John's moving force as long as he could remember.
His parents had been slaveholders and had died together in an
accident, perhaps, or in whatever way people met sudden death
in Virginia in 1832. John was brought to his uncle's lavish
household on an inland plantation in southwestern Virginia.
A tutor came to teach him and his cousin—older than himself
and belonging to that other world—the world of white grown-
ups. From his earliest days he wanted no part of it.

Bill, a slave on the uncle's plantation, was three years
older than John. It was Bill who took him blackberrying and
on secret excursions across the fields to watch the railroad
being built. Tracks going on and on, out of their sight, like
fingers pointing "Go!" All the way to something Bill called
Canada or North or Freedom.

At ten Bill was put in the field to hoe tobacco, and the
only times John could see him were Sundays or nights if
he slipped out of bed and down to the quarters. At fifteen,
all Bill's talk, whenever the two got together, was of running
away. It was fun to think up ways a person could escape
from the Fairfield plantation. But it wasn't until John was
eighteen that they got around to doing anything about it.

Then one evening John announced at the supper table
that he thought he'd like to settle out in Ohio or Indiana
or somewhere in the West. They might as well stop planning
for him to enter the university. He thought he'd be leaving
on the next Monday morning. What he didn't announce
was that Bill would also be leaving, in the dark of Sunday
night, on one of the horses out of the pasture.

"Ten horses wouldn't pay for all the work you've done,"
John had said when Bill hesitated about taking the horse.
"Besides, when a man's liberty has been stolen, he has a right
to take anything to get it back." He had handed Bill a

pass to carry in his pocket, signed John Fairfield, owner; to make it look legal he carried in his own pocket a forged deed.

John took off early on a bright October morning and he thought he'd never seen the woods more glorious—all scarlet and yellow below the dark pines. He met Bill at the appointed tobacco barn, and the two rode through the hills of western Virginia and through Pennsylvania and Ohio all the way to the Canadian border. They trotted their horses across the line and let out a whoop of sheer ecstasy, two free young men in the beautiful world of freedom. Then they took turns tearing the forged papers into pieces no bigger than snow-flakes and tossing them into the air like confetti.

The ecstasy lasted a little over twenty-four hours. By the time the town of Windsor came into sight, Bill was grieving for all the others they had had to leave behind—the cook and the old man who prayed every night for an end to slavery. And the twins—Tiny and Jim.

John knew how he felt. His own mind had been running the same way, not for any special people but for all the four million wasting their lives in bondage.

"All right," he announced to Bill a few days later, "I'll go bring the rest of them out. I'll figure a way."

He'd been talking to the people in the colony at Windsor and had learned things he hadn't dreamed of. He had found out that there was an Underground Railroad. Twenty thousand people had got out through the Underground just this year—not counting Bill. There were conductors with maps and hideaway stations and compasses—and guns. There were regular stationmasters of the free side too—William Still in Philadelphia, and in Cincinnati there were Mr. Hatfield and the Quaker, Levi Coffin, who was the "president" of the Underground Railroad.

"He's a white Southerner, like you," one of the ex-slaves

had explained. "From North Carolina. Been in the Underground work since before you was born, I reckon."

Fairfield went back as far as he could by train, in a hurry to bring out Bill's friends as he'd promised. He found that his uncle had a warrant out for his arrest for slave stealing, so he couldn't go near the plantation. But he got word to the cook, and on the appointed night she brought eighteen of his uncle's slaves to the meeting place. John was there ahead of time with a canvas-covered wagon—the kind hundreds of people were buying to go out to the West. He had forged papers for each of the fugitives to carry on his person and drove mainly through woods at night just to be on the safe side until they could find a way across the Ohio River and to Levi Coffin's house. John didn't have enough money to get all eighteen to Canada and he needed the Quaker's advice.

The old man and his wife invited the fugitives right through the front door into the parlor. And when it was mealtime, they all ate together. The Coffins were the first white people John Fairfield ever admired.

Levi Coffin didn't know what to make of John. Here was a young man who cheerfully told of stealing horses (or anything else necessary) to bring slaves to freedom; a young man who insisted that fugitives should be armed and prepared to fight off any attacker; who saw the Underground as a kind of guerrilla war against slave owners. Coffin, a businessman and a Quaker, had the greatest respect for property, though he delighted in outwitting slave owners and slave catchers. He shook his head over Fairfield's escapades—but as time passed he found himself waiting eagerly for word of Fairfield brought by fugitives John sent, and even more eagerly for the rare visits of the young Virginian himself.

In the three years since their first meeting, John had come to know Coffin well and also many others from North and South who were devoting much of their time to the movement.

They all had families or homes or jobs. John had none of these; his mind, his exuberant, somewhat wild spirit was fired with a hatred of the system of slavery and what he could do to end it.

When John made his trip to Canada with his uncle's slaves, he had found Bill married and settled down. Other fugitives in the colony were awaiting his arrival. They had scraped together four hundred dollars and they begged him to go South again to bring out their relatives. A wife, a husband, a brother, a father who had sent his three sons out years ago . . . How could John refuse?

He warned them that it would take time. So far he had depended on luck. From now on there would be no reckless adventuring. He would plan carefully and use their money wisely. From now on, like John Brown, like Harriet Tubman and the hundreds of nameless ones, he was a Railroad man.

John Fairfield had the zest of a Robin Hood. He became an artist in camouflaging his purpose. Sometimes he acted alone; often he had teammates, chosen as a rule from among the free black men in Cincinnati. They acted parts as "body servants" or as slaves or as stablemen. Like John they took various names and disguises. He delighted in arranging imaginative roles for the fugitives. Boys became old men, women became boys for the journey.

Sometimes John posed as a rough and ready slave trader, or a peddler going to the back doors with his wagon full of bright cloth, pins, needles, enticing statuary. He went in this way all through Tennessee and Alabama, hiding slaves under false-bottom boards in the daytime, finding quiet spots where they could sleep under the stars at night.

Once he was jailed for two months and escaped just before his trial, vowing to free a slave for every day he was in prison. Shortly afterward he had carried through an elaborate plot with two accomplices at a saltworks, pretending to be the outraged victim of his own plots.

Often John would go into a rich plantation area, arrange to stay at one of the big houses, proclaim himself pro-slavery as expected of a Virginia gentleman. Being a guest in the household made it easy to communicate with the slaves he intended to rescue. This was the scheme he had used to get in contact with Marsh.

But conducting Marsh to free soil did not end with the day in the Kentucky cave. The country was in even greater turmoil than John had expected. It took the party of twelve strong men two weeks to battle their way through to the northern shore of the Ohio. When the wounded, battered crew dragged themselves to Levi Coffin's home, the Quaker opened his door at once, though he didn't until minutes later recognize John among the fugitives.

"A posse was lying in ambush at the end of a bridge," John explained. "When we got fairly on the bridge they fired at us from each end. Thought no doubt the sudden attack would force us to surrender. They made a mistake. I ordered the men to charge. And charge they did. We fired as we ran and the men in ambush scattered like scared sheep."

"You might have killed someone," said Coffin, a man of peace.

For an answer Fairfield pulled back his sleeve and showed the torn flesh on his arm. He pointed out several bullet holes in his grimy clothes. "Peter Wells has a more serious wound. We were in close quarters. We shot to kill and we made the slave-hunting devils run."

"But killing is wrong." Levi Coffin made the gentle reproof even as he washed John's wounds. "It is better to suffer wrong than to do wrong. We must love our enemies."

John looked into the Quaker's troubled eyes. He wished he could make him understand.

"When I undertake to conduct slaves out of bondage," he said slowly, "I feel it my duty to defend them to the last drop of my blood."

The man of peace did not answer. He gave up preaching his principles to the worn young Virginian. He knew John would fight for the fugitives as long as his life lasted.

After this episode, the Coffins did not see John for a long time, but parties of fugitives from Alabama and Tennessee, Kentucky and Virginia came to their door, sent by Fairfield.

The last time Levi Coffin saw John was when he brought a group of twenty-eight slaves up from Kentucky. He led the party—men and women and children and one baby a few months old—to the Ohio opposite the mouth of the Big Miami, where he knew there were several skiffs tied to the bank near a woodyard. All twenty-nine people squeezed into three skiffs. The overloaded boats rode deep in the water. A few hundred feet from the Ohio shore, the boat in which John was riding began to sink. He jumped out and tried to pull the boat to shore through shallow water. In a moment he had sunk to his waist in quicksand and mud. Only the strong brown arms of the fugitives kept him from drowning. Together they managed to get the boat close enough to the shore so that the entire party could wade in. They reached land, soaking wet and without a pair of shoes among them.

It was pouring rain and the weather was cold. Shivering, hungry, with bruised, lacerated feet, they reached the outskirts of Cincinnati and hid in the outlying ravines. Fairfield crept through town at dawn, evading the ever-present slave catchers, to reach John Hatfield's house.

Mrs. Hatfield gave him dry clothes and made him eat some breakfast while her husband went to get several of the Negro abolitionist leaders and Levi and Katy Coffin. John paced the floor while they made hasty plans. They would hire a hearse, a couple of funeral coaches and a few buggies from a German livery stable where the proprietor never asked Friend Coffin too many questions. They could go out the road past the ravines toward Mill Creek and along the road to the burying ground "for colored."

After they passed the cemetery, one buggy would ride ahead and bring the word to Jonathan Cable, the Underground stationmaster up at College Hill. The refugees could hide in the Negro community until Cable and Coffin worked out the rest of the itinerary. The authorities would not stop a solemn funeral procession.

Mr. Hatfield drove the hearse which was crammed with fugitives inside. White-gloved mourners (fugitives, too) flanked the procession. John and Levi and Katy Coffin brought up the rear in a buggy. But what had been a merry farce turned to tragedy at College Hill. The three-month-old baby had died—so quietly that no one knew it.

A little grave was dug and the baby buried in Jonathan Cable's back yard. "In freedom," the mother whispered.

But to John Fairfield the death of the child was a blow. He was ill besides. The cough that he had had so long racked his whole body. Katy Coffin took a look at him and bundled him home and to bed. He didn't recover with his usual speed and listened at last to Coffin's persuasions that he give up the life of a conductor and settle down.

A friend of Coffin's in Randolph County, Indiana, offered to set John up with a stock of goods for a store in a settlement of free Negroes. He kept store for almost a year and a half until the middle of October 1859.

The news traveled over the country of John Brown's raid on the arsenal at Harpers Ferry, the failure of his plan to arm the slaves for insurrection, the old man's capture. John read every scrap of news he could get, eavesdropped on every conversation on the other side of his store counter. He said very little, but sometime between Brown's capture and his trial he walked out of the store and disappeared.

At first none of his friends worried. Levi Coffin, when he heard John was gone, guessed he was in Canada. The people in Windsor thought he was still keeping store in Randolph County. Letters went back and forth but no more was heard of his whereabouts. Fugitives coming to Coffin's Underground station had heard nothing, though one group mentioned a white man with a peddler's wagon who had led some friends of theirs through Tennessee.

Then in the fall of 1860, just a few months before the Civil War broke out, Coffin read in a newspaper of an insurrectionary movement among slaves near an ironworks on the Cumberland River in Tennessee. Several fugitives who attempted to defend themselves were shot. The rest were captured and hanged. Among those who were hanged by the mob was a white man thought to be between twenty-five and thirty years old.

Coffin guessed that it was Fairfield who was killed. By Quaker standards John had been a wicked man. But Coffin said of him, "He was an inveterate hater of slavery, and this alone motivated every action of his whole life. With all his faults and misguided impulses, he was a brave man; he never betrayed a trust that was reposed in him, and he was a true friend to the oppressed and suffering slave."

How could John Fairfield have betrayed a trust placed in him by a slave who longed to be free? To free himself from the chains that scarred his spirit, John Fairfield had to break the chains that held the bodies of his darker brothers.

# Soldier's 5 choice

"I believe this government cannot endure permanently half slave and half free," Abraham Lincoln had said in 1858. And he had raised a question, "You say slavery is wrong. But don't you constantly argue, 'This is not the right place to oppose it?' It must not be opposed in politics, because that will raise a fuss; it must not be opposed in the pulpit, because it is not religion. Then where is the place to oppose it?"

In April 1861, barely a month after Lincoln's inauguration as President of the United States, in the shots fired on Fort Sumter, he had his answer.

The question of slavery and the extension of slavery, the question of the very existence of the Union, were to be decided on the battlefield.

"We must abandon compromise," secessionist leaders from Alabama declared. And Lincoln called for 75,000 volunteers "to put down rebellion."

But the struggle was no simple matter of putting down rebellion. It was a civil war, based on the sectional question of human freedom. Without slavery there would have been no armed conflict, but, the Union and the States' rights question of division of power between State and Federal government also entered in. Many Americans in the South were opposed to the system of slavery. Many—probably a majority—in the North were not ready to go to war to free Negro slaves. Abraham Lincoln could not have won support for the conflict without his firm stand that the nation was at war to save the Union and the Constitution.

The questions raised by war were easy only for the slave-holding class in the South, shouting "States' rights" and meaning the right to keep human beings in perpetual bondage; and for the dedicated abolitionists among whom were numbered every Negro American, North or South, slave or free. Others were faced with a heartbreaking choice of loyalties.

At the beginning there was one class of men for whom the choice was especially difficult. These were Southern-born officers in the United States Army and Navy, and their number was far out of proportion to the population of the Confederate states. Among the Southern navy men was Admiral David Glasgow Farragut, born near Knoxville, Tennessee. Until he was twelve years old his home was in the South, in Knoxville and then New Orleans. The rest of his eventful life, until the opening of the Civil War, was spent wholly upon the sea. Perhaps for this reason and because he was strongly opposed to slavery, Farragut seems to have had no hesitancy about his allegiance on the side of the Union.

Two hundred and eighty-nine other Southerners among the officers in the Navy also chose to remain at their posts in the service of the United States. There was a reason. Free Negroes had served on navy ships since the days of the Revolution. Mess and quarters were by tradition shared by all, regardless of race or color. In the first year of the Civil War one fourth of the sailors were free Negroes. In such an atmosphere, a war to perpetuate slavery would have small attraction to officers or men.

The regular Army was a different matter. It was officered by men trained at the Military Academy at West Point, New York. Though situated in the North, the Academy's traditions and its whole outlook were those of the Southern planter class. In the years when the slavery question was agitating the nation, the head of the Academy and many of the instructors were from slaveholding families in the South. It was natural that many of the cadets should be imbued with the pro-slavery ideas of their instructors. Abolitionist agitation became a subject for ridicule. In 1861 the War Department called all officers to duty and the governors of the eleven states in the Confederacy called them home "to defend the land from invaders."

With families in the home state, with the affection people have for the earth, the trees, the hills and valleys they have roamed as children, it took something strong to keep these men on the side of the Union. Yet eighty-six made this choice. Six became generals in the Federal armies, all fought well for the Union throughout the war. Among the volunteers who formed and led companies from the West were also many "exiles" with Southern backgrounds.

A good many illiterate backwoodsmen along the border left family and friends to make their way to the Federal armies to enlist, or to act as guides and scouts for troops as spies.

Why did these white Southern loyalists choose to be branded as traitors to their home place? Why brave the doubts and suspicions they met within the Federal lines? For the Stars and Stripes on a battlefield and the history it stood for? For the image of a backwoodsman in the White House, struggling to save the Union? Probably each one acted from mixed motives. Surely there were a few who, willing to support the Union, were also willing to perpetuate slavery. Surely there were many determined to end the system, who found in war a way to speak out for human freedom.

# George Henry Thomas

A ten-year-old boy on a bay horse rode through the gates of the park surrounding his home. He skirted the veranda of the two-story brick house and rode on to the stables where he was met by a barefoot stable boy, about his age but half his size. Holding on to the bridle, the small Negro asked in a low voice, "Do we git to go to the grove today, Marse George?"

George Thomas dismounted and lifted a green baize bag of books off the horn of the saddle. "I guess so, Araisi."

Ever since he had started school at the Southampton Academy last fall, George had made it a practice to gather the half dozen boys on the plantation in a maple grove in back of the alfalfa field and repeat for them the lessons he had learned that day. They had no books except the one he kept in his own hand and no blackboard, like at school, to write letters or numbers. His scholars traced words in the dust under the trees with their fingers or with a twig off a branch. You couldn't learn very much that way. Even so, George's father, when he ran across the "grove school," had objected pretty strenuously.

He spoke of it that night at the dinner table (the other children still ate in the nursery, but George, being the oldest son, had the privilege of dining with his parents when there were no guests). In Virginia in the year 1826 the laws against teaching slaves were not always enforced but Mr. Thomas had his own ideas on the subject. Reading and writing were the ruination of blacks. They put ideas in their heads. All a slave had to learn was obedience.

"But, Father"—George stuttered a little in his earnestness—"they like for-for me to teach them. It's not *just* to keep Araisi and the rest from g-getting education."

"Just" was a word that would be often on his lips through his lifetime.

"Nonsense."

Gently, George's mother, across the table, intervened.

"Can a child playing at being teacher do any real harm, my dear?"

Teaching the boys on the plantation was not a childish game to the serious-minded boy. He worried about his father's disapproval, but he kept right on with the lessons for another year. Not every day, of course, and most often when Mr. Thomas was out hunting or had ridden over to one of his other plantations so he wouldn't be offended by the sight of his slaves looking over his son's shoulder to see how a line of reading looked in a book. George hated to go against his tall, handsome father, but you had to do what you thought was—just.

Then, when George was eleven, his father fell from his horse, jumping a ditch in a fox hunt, and was killed. The boy was deeply shocked; he took the death as a sort of terrible punishment and he never taught the young slaves again.

Still later, when he was sixteen, there was a dreadful slave uprising in the next county, and his mother and all the family had to go into a blockhouse in town for a night for protection.

And everybody said that Nat Turner had got the idea of murdering his master from reading about Egypt and Pharaoh in the Bible. So new, strict laws were passed against teaching slaves to read.

George wasn't convinced that you had the right to keep the people who were your responsibility in ignorance; but he was occupied with helping his mother direct the affairs of the plantation until at nineteen he went into town to live with his uncle and begin the study of law. Quite soon the study of law was interrupted by a chance to go to West Point. The decision was left to him.

George Thomas was mature for his years, over six feet, with bright blue eyes, light brown, wavy hair, full lips and a jutting, purposeful chin. His carriage was already that of a military man. An old man at the courthouse had once told him that he looked like George Washington. This, secretly, gave him a good deal of pleasure, because Washington was one of his heroes. To be a soldier from Virginia, to defend the country Virginians had done so much to build, appealed to his imagination. He accepted the appointment to the military academy.

Life at West Point suited him. The hard work, the discipline, the chance to excel stimulated his mind. Most of the cadets were from prominent Southern families much like his own, but it happened that his roommate was a Vermonter and his best friend a red-haired, undisciplined frontiersman from Ohio, "Cump" Sherman. William Tecumseh Sherman was only sixteen, somewhat wild and rough-mannered. It was perhaps the contrast between the three young plebes that drew them into a friendship. There were long three-sided talks in the dark after taps, the kind of growing-up talk that helps young people know their own minds.

Stewart Van Vliet, the Vermonter, was twenty-one, and after his eight years of study and service in the Army he meant to be a clergyman. He was interested in the problem of Negro slavery and had been brought up to believe that holding a human soul in bondage was wrong. Cump, whose foster father was a United States senator, had spent some time in Washington, a Southern city in every respect. It was his opinion that the whole question could best be left in the hands of Southern statesmen. "If it wasn't for the blacks, how would they have the leisure time to run the government?" George, a product of this dear-bought leisure, was inclined to agree with Stewart—there was no justice in the slave system. But there it was, as old as any institution in the country.

There wasn't any reason to abuse the Negroes who worked

Though in the North, West Point was permeated with Southern traditions.

for you, he said. The lash should go, and all the other cruelties. And the blacks had a right to education—reading and writing, at the least. He told his friends about the time he taught the slave boys in the maple grove. George hadn't thought of the grove school for years, but in the quiet darkness of the austere room at the academy he took a certain pleasure in remembering it. It hadn't done any harm, he added. His mother never had any trouble with her Negroes.

That first year it was still possible to carry on a calm conversation between friends about the subject. Before the end of their term at West Point, in 1840, opinion had hardened over the country. The only acceptable attitude at West Point was ridicule of the long-haired abolitionists who were wrecking the nation. George Thomas still held his moderate opinion but he didn't press it. West Point was a world of its own, with study and drilling between reveille and taps and, in the late night, the worry of how to advance in rank when you went into the Army. With the country *almost* at peace there was small chance of winning promotion or glory.

Keeping the Indians in check in the West was too easy. There was only the small Florida war against the Seminoles. That had dragged on for years but it was the best assignment to be hoped for.

After a few months of routine service, the young officer had the "luck" to be sent to St. Augustine, under the command of Zachary Taylor. But he was in charge of the commissary and also acted as adjutant, and was too piled up with detailed work at the fort to do any fighting. Furthermore he found that the fighting consisted mainly of hunting fugitive slaves who had attached themselves to the Indian villages. Still, as he wrote a fellow classmate from West Point:

"This will be the only opportunity I shall have of distinguishing myself, and not to be able to avail myself of it is too bad."

What the West Pointers in their isolation hadn't realized was the turmoil in the minds of slaveholders. The demand for cotton for export to British factories was enormous, and the land in the cotton states was wearing thin. Africans were being smuggled in freely, but where could they be used? The new territories in the Northwest were no good for growing cotton and besides were being organized by New Englanders and foreigners who had no intention of permitting slavery. There was Texas, on the Mexican border, independent but anxious to become a part of the United States. And not just Texas but a whole wealth of unsettled land that Mexicans had no use for. . . . The Southern aristocrats would lose their control of the government unless new states could be brought into the Union at the South. They had found the Army quite useful in clearing out the hiding places of runaway slaves in the Florida Everglades. In a war with Mexico, the soldiers would be serving a greater need.

It took a little time to whip up a war, but in 1846, Santa Anna, the Mexican revolutionist, gave a good excuse. First Lieutenant George Thomas found himself in command of a battery of artillery in General Taylor's army. He had his opportunity for glory and promotion at the Battle of Buena Vista. By his skill and courage against the Mexicans, Thomas helped save the day in that important engagement. For this he was promoted. After victory was won, he went home on furlough. The citizens of his own country presented him with a handsome sword with the names of the battles in which he participated inscribed on the scabbard.

A bona fide hero, he was sent to teach at West Point. It was at this stay at West Point that Captain Thomas met and married Frances Kellogg of Troy, New York. This was a most fortunate marriage. Frances was both beautiful and intelligent. She looked up to "Thom" as a war hero, and shared his thinking on every important subject. Her sympathy was to be a rock of strength in the difficult times looming on the horizon. They had a year together before Thomas was sent on a tour of duty to California.

The gold rush was at its height, but George Thomas, stationed on a reservation of Yuma Indians, spent his time studying their language—as he had spent spare hours on the Mexican border studying Spanish. He had an interest and respect for all the people who made up America. In 1855 he was ordered from California to Texas as a major in the 2nd Cavalry. This was the regiment Jefferson Davis, then Secretary of War and soon to become President of the Confederacy, had thoughtfully organized as a way to gather together the best of the Southern-born West Pointers.

The officers' mess at the headquarters was like a little country club. Every one of the men had been at West Point at the same time, either as instructors or cadets. They were from different states, but from the same upper-class slave-owning background. The atmosphere was charged with tension. Major Thomas (who was the last to arrive) found his friends reading hometown papers. Not only reading them, but sharing them and discussing what the South would do if the people elected the "Black Republican" candidate as President.

"If Lincoln is elected," one of his friends quoted a Georgia senator as saying, "the citizens will wake up next morning to find they have no country for him to preside over."

With approval, his fellow officers noted that South Carolina was proposing to arm every man between the ages of eighteen and forty-five and was calling for enrollment of volunteers. They would need officers. "Unfurl the Palmetto flag and fling it to the breeze. With the spirit of a brave man, live and die as did his glorious ancestors and ring notes of defiance in the ears of an insolent foe." Statesmen made handsome speeches.

When Thomas questioned the wisdom of these threats, someone pointed to the words of Mr. Ruffin, a neighbor in

Virginia: "Let the first drop of blood be spilled on the soil of South Carolina! It will bring Virginia and every Southern state to her side."

George was troubled. Did they really expect war? Did they welcome secession? Even before the first vote was cast in the national election? These friends of his had taken a solemn oath of allegiance to defend the United States and its flag—as he had himself.

He was very tired, and when it happened that he suffered a slight wound—an arrow thrust received in a skirmish with a small body of Indians—he decided that he would ask for a leave of absence from the Army, a long leave. He needed to get away and think things out. He left the regiment and started North in October 1860, five days before election.

Going through Virginia on the way to New York to join his wife, the soldier met with another accident, this one more serious. The train had stopped outside of Norfolk to change engines. To step out a moment on Virginia soil, to breathe the night air, sweet with honeysuckle, was a temptation. But the step was high and George fell heavily and injured his spine.

Taken into Norfolk, he sent for Frances, and when, after a month, he could be moved, they went to his mother's, to the spacious, beautiful house where he had been brought up and where the family—all of it—still lived. His young sisters, his brother Benjamin, who had been a long-legged teen-ager the last time he'd been home on furlough, all were there, all grown-up. Benjamin was married to a quiet dark-haired girl, the daughter of a neighbor.

The family was elated to see their hero brother home again. It was almost as if he were the first-wounded in the coming war. Because he was certain, Benjamin said, that war would come. Lincoln's inauguration was just a couple of months away. South Carolina had already seceded and had called home her officers from the Army to defend the state. It was too bad the legislature at Richmond was so slow. "Virginia ought to act in time to send delegates to the big show in Alabama. I hear they're going to call our new government the Confederate States of America."

George winced. His back was very painful and he used the pain as an excuse to keep from answering Ben. He was slow to recover. The turmoil of events didn't help his health. Frances tried to shield him from the war talk that was mounting in excitement, as the papers brought news of state after state seceding from the Union. She tried without success to find cheerful items to read in papers that came to her from New York. The Southern members of President Buchanan's cabinet had resigned and gone home, she read. So had the senators. But the members of the House stayed on and were making such violent and insulting speeches she wouldn't show the papers to her husband. George was fighting a battle in his own mind in silence.

Frances Thomas knew what his family expected. The sword the county had given George hung over the desk in the corner, and every time his mother came into the room Frances saw the older woman's eyes linger proudly over its polished scabbard. If Virginia seceded from the Union, if there was war, her eldest son would bring honor to the Thomas name fighting in defense of their lands, their country, their home—and their "property in Negroes."

February came and went, and the Confederacy was a grim reality. George's back was well enough for him to be up and about. He could mount a horse, and together he and Frances rode over the plantation. Past the slave quarters, past the fields ready for the planting in tobacco, across the meadow and through the grove where he had once taught reading to slave boys. Because it had been *just*—and because they had loved to learn. Together, on the day after the fourth of March, they read the sad, painfully thought-out conciliatory words the new President spoke at his inauguration:

"The Union is perpetual, confirmed by the history of the Union itself. The Union is much older than the Constitution. It was formed in fact by the Articles of Association in 1774. It was matured and continued by the Declaration of Independence . . . and the Constitution. It follows, from these views, that no State can lawfully get out of the Union. . . ."

Then, addressing himself to the citizens of the states in rebellion, Lincoln had said, "In your hands, my dissatisfied fellow-countrymen, and not in mine, is the momentous issue of Civil War. . . . *You* have no oath registered in Heaven to destroy the Government, while I shall have the most solemn one to preserve, protect and defend it. . . ."

Frances folded the paper and put it away. A few days later she returned North alone. She did not want to influence George in the hard decision he would have to make.

Still Virginia hesitated, though the governor sent out a summons to the officers in the Federal Army to come to the defense of the home state. George Thomas stayed on the plantation with his family until two days before Fort Sumter was fired on. Then he wrote a note to his wife, telling her his decision: "Whichever way I turn it over in my mind, my oath of allegiance to the government always comes uppermost."

His mother called him a traitor to his face. His sisters would not even say good-by. Benjamin ran sobbing from the room when he saw George take his sword from the wall and strap it to his side. His journey carried him North, through Richmond, which would within a month become the capital of the Confederacy. He went by ferry across the Potomac to Washington for orders. He never saw his home in Virginia again.

The War Department in Washington appeared surprised to see the tall, imposing figure of the Major of Artillery, 2nd

Cavalry, U. S. Army. All the other staff officers of that regiment had resigned. The regiment, without officers, without horses, without guns, had been ordered unceremoniously out of Texas. The base was in Confederate hands. The leaderless regiment was stationed in Carlisle, Pennsylvania. Major Thomas was ordered there at once to re-equip and whip it back into shape. But there was no warm welcome for the Virginian. As a Southerner from a slaveholding family he was looked on with suspicion. From the beloved home he would never see, he came to isolation where he could rightly have expected a hero's welcome.

William Tecumseh Sherman got wind of the fact that the loyalty of his old friend was being questioned. Even the President doubted whether Major Thomas would be able to fight with a whole heart against his own people! Sherman went to him and said, "Mr. Lincoln, he is as loyal as I am and as a soldier superior to most on your list of generals."

Lincoln asked, "Will you be responsible for him?"

"With the greatest pleasure," Sherman replied.

But after he had spoken, Sherman began to worry. He hadn't seen George for several years. What if the judgment he had made was wrong? He heard that the 2nd Cavalry was stationed a few miles from Washington in Maryland and went there to give the situation a second look.

The two talked personalities a few minutes before Sherman asked bluntly, "George, there are some doubts about your loyalty? Which way are you going?"

"I'm going South," George answered dryly and, taking note of the look of alarm on Sherman's face, added slowly, "You need give yourself no worry, Cump. I am going South—with my men."

George Thomas defied his Southern heritage to fight for the Union in the Civil War.

Go South, George Thomas did, fighting his way through the heart of the Confederacy for four years. Promotions came slowly however—there were still those in the War Department who found it hard to forget that he was Southern born.

All during the war, General Thomas was one of the loneliest men in America. The epithets of *poltroon,* of *slave stealer,* of *traitor* hurled at him in the Southern press had grieved him greatly. He had not even been notified when his mother died. Being cut off forever from his family was a deep sadness. An even harder blow had been the unjust doubts of his loyalty to the Union cause. Though by the close of the war these doubts were dispelled, he could not forget.

"There is one thing about my promotions that is exceedingly gratifying," he said. "I never received a promotion they dared withhold."

Three things, however, kept him from being embittered. First was the devotion of those who served under him—from the 2nd Cavalry men he led in the first weeks of combat to the company of Negro soldiers from Kansas in the Nashville campaign in '64; second, the unfailing pride and trust of his wife; and third, his own knowledge that he had done his duty in a cause that was just.

It cannot be said that General Thomas subjected himself to being branded a traitor for the *sole* purpose of freeing the slaves. He is numbered among white freedom-loving Southerners because of his superb military contribution to victory. If he had been less sensitive to the opinion of the defeated slaveholders, if his understanding of the needs of the country had equaled his devotion to it, he might have used the knowledge given to him by his Southern background to provide leadership in winning an enduring peace. At the close of the war he was asked to go to New Orleans to direct the reconstruction of that area. He refused the assignment on the grounds that the "hostility of the people toward me makes it impossible for me to be of any service in endeavoring to reconstruct the Southern states."

What he could not realize was that the hostility was felt only by a *part* of the Southern people. In 1870 (shortly after George Thomas' sudden death in San Francisco) a teacher in a Freedmen's Bureau school near Southampton, Virginia, was interviewing literate Negroes in the neighborhood who might be able to instruct others. A middle-aged carpenter offered his services. His name, he said, was Araisi Givens.

He'd been teaching as best he could without any books, since emancipation. "General Thomas taught me reading and writing," he explained. "Colored people think a great deal of General Thomas around here."

# Freedom
# 6 to the free

In 1861 at Fortress Monroe, Virginia, a Confederate officer came with a flag of truce to demand the return of three slaves who had escaped and taken refuge in the camp of the Union soldiers. To the demand General Benjamin Butler replied, "Since under Virginia law, slaves are property and under the laws of war, property of the enemy is properly subject to confiscation, I shall detain the Negroes as contraband." The Confederate officer went away empty-handed.

Contraband! A strange term to apply to living human beings seeking freedom! At the very opening of hostilities the enslaved Negroes had looked on the United States' soldiers as liberators, and when Butler's decision became accepted policy by the War Department, emancipation may be said to have begun. Walking great distances on foot, rowing through the night in stolen skiffs, slipping through the woods by secret paths or galloping on horseback down the road to freedom, fugitives appeared at every army post and declared themselves "contraband." A year before the first free Negro soldier was enrolled in the fighting forces, two years before the Emancipation Proclamation, almost a hundred thousand former slaves were being fed and clothed and being given the rough beginning of an education behind the Union lines. As hostlers, foragers for food, cooks, nurses for the wounded, scouts and spies they made themselves exceedingly useful.

At the war's end, out of the "Department for Care of the

Negro" set up by the Army, came the Freedmen's Bureau, to deal with the grave problems of adjustment between the former masters and the former slaves. The long fight against the system of slavery begun by leaders of the American Revolution, carried on by the abolitionists, self-exiled from Southern soil, by the conductors of the Underground Railroad, by the two hundred thousand black soldiers in the Union Army at the close of the war, was over. Now began the struggle for full citizenship and equality with white Americans to the one eighth of the population denied it—an eighth largely located in the conquered South.

Making peace after war is never easy. The removal by assassination of a wise leader skilled in conciliation made the task doubly difficult. "In giving freedom to the slave, we give freedom to the free," Lincoln had said. And just before he died he proclaimed amnesty to all—except a few rebel leaders— who would take an oath to uphold the Constitution and the laws and proclamations touching slavery. Speaking to Negroes of Richmond, Virginia, even before the Confederate Army had surrendered, Lincoln praised the twelve thousand voters in Louisiana who were reorganizing their state, "giving the benefit of free public schools to black and white alike and empowering their legislature to confer the elective franchise upon the colored man." These were the acts he expected and hoped for from the Southerners as they voted themselves back into the Union.

But four years of devastating war had not prepared the South for the necessary steps to real freedom for former slaves. For the most part they accepted the fact that bodily possession of chattel slaves and of their children and their children's children must be given up. What they would not—could not— grasp was that emancipation implied citizenship and equality of Americans with dark skins. Instead of schools and suffrage for the freedmen, they tried to set up new constitutions with new Black Codes for governing the Negro, making him a slave again in everything but name.

Negroes knew what they wanted, what was necessary if their condition was to be changed. In every state they gathered in meetings and drew up petitions to the government. Some of the petitions were couched in half-illiterate language. Some were marked by eloquence. The meaning of all the petitions was clear: "We ask for a citizenship so solid that upon it black men, white men and every American born can equally, safely and eternally stand."

They wanted, they said, to stay in the states where they had been born. They asked for land or work for wages, for education and the right to vote, to testify in law courts, to bear arms and for the elimination of all discrimination based on color. In these reasonable demands they were supported by most of the Army generals whom Congress had put in command, by the teachers and nurses and ministers who had come as volunteers from the North as agents of the Freedmen's Bureau.

In 1867, a reconstruction plan was put forward by the Federal Government. The Fourteenth and Fifteenth Amendments to the Constitution were passed, guaranteeing to the freedmen full protection of the laws of state as well as nation, and providing that the right of suffrage should not be denied because of race, color or previous condition of servitude. The states which had been in rebellion were placed under military control until they drew up new state constitutions in accordance with the new amendments.

Under the Reconstruction Act, those who had led the rebellion were disfranchised. Many others of the old landed aristocracy refrained from taking any part in the government and kept aloof from the teachers and Freedmen's Bureau men from the North, men they termed "carpetbaggers."

However, among the planters in every state there were a few men who had long deplored the institution of slavery and were resigned to its end. They were willing to undertake the

Carpetbaggers, scalawags and newly enfranchised Negroes set up democratic state governments.

responsibility of forming a new government in company with men they had held as chattels. In addition many white farmers and artisans found themselves able to vote for the first time. All these, the aristocrats lumped together under the contemptuous name of "scalawags."

Carpetbaggers, scalawags and the newly enfranchised Negroes met together to set up democratic state governments that would restore the shattered economy, rebuild ruined cities and establish a new and more humane society.

Over the whole South they established, for the first time, free public schools. They provided relief for poor laborers; built orphan asylums and institutions for the deaf and dumb and insane. They instituted a more nearly just form of taxation, abolished property qualifications for holding office and made it possible for small farmers, Negro and white, to buy unused land. They restored roads and bridges and railroads.

The Negroes could not have achieved the success they did without the votes of the scalawags. Scalawags, especially the poorer class, voted against all forms of bigotry. History has ignored these men. Even when their names are known, there has been small recognition for their courage and honesty in resisting the general scorn and contempt for any white who associated himself with the former slaves. The Reconstruction legislatures lasted no longer than ten years; a long time would go by before political power in proportion to their numbers would come into the hands of Southerners with dark skins again.

# James Hunnicutt

"Property" had turned into human beings and tramped the highway in a never-ending, ragged, motley procession. Week-days or Sunday seemed to make no difference. The exodus of the emancipated had gone on for months in the wake of the Yankee army as it moved across Virginia to besiege Richmond, then its numbers had dwindled to a mere trickle. Now it had started like a tidal wave at the news of the surrender at Appomattox Courthouse.

To the congregation in the red brick church at a crossroads in Fredericksburg, the sound of squeaky wagon wheels and shuffling bare feet was a torture. Their own slaves were long gone. Heaven knows where these blacks had come from, or where they thought they were going, breaking the quiet of the Sabbath.

The Reverend James Hunnicutt, in the pulpit, raised his voice above the din and cheerfully called for a hymn: *Praise God from Whom All Blessings Flow*. His cheerfulness was an insult. What was one to think of a minister who in the month of April 1865, in Fredericksburg, Virginia, had no more decency than to pray for that abomination of an abolitionist in the White House in Washington and to follow his prayer with that hymn? Someone hissed and one of the elders flung down his hymn book and stalked out. There was an outraged stampede for the door.

James Hunnicutt stared at the empty pews and through the church door swinging open at God's sunlight outside. He was a minister of the gospel but he was no Christ to say: "Forgive them, Father, they know not what they do." Yet he did feel a sort of pity for these unrepentant whites who could not see that in rejecting freedom for the slaves they were rejecting a larger freedom for themselves. Nevertheless he hated their hypocrisy, their talk of how they loved their Negroes until emancipation came. Then it was, "The Yankees freed you, let the Yankees feed you." They had let them leave empty-handed, with nothing they could call their own after years of unpaid labor. Driving the freedmen away, yet resenting their going, casting abuse and ridicule on their joy in freedom. Well, he was proud to be cast out, too.

This was not the first church Hunnicutt had lost. Five years earlier, when the first secession talk began in his native South

Carolina, Hunnicutt owned three slaves—one, a woman who cooked for him at the parsonage. (To this day he winced to remember that he had bought her cheap from one of his parishioners because she was lame.) The second was an old man he had inherited from his fisherman father. The third was Jeff, a strapping fellow who also served as sexton of the church. James had grown up believing or at least parroting the thought that "Providence had appointed South Carolina to be worked by black slaves because of the hot climate which Negroes were better used to than white people." Had not John Wesley, founder of his Methodist denomination, said that bringing the Africans to America was a positive good because it offered the heathen the chance of breeding their posterity in the knowledge of the Lord?

He had believed in spite of the evidence of the whipping post and the Black Codes that there was a peculiarity in the love masters entertained for their slaves that did not apply to other pieces of property. Certainly he loved his servants—or did he? Had he ever once considered their natures as human beings?

An abolitionist tract picked up off the street one day, when the authorities were burning a shipment from the mailboat, had started this line of thinking. The edges of the paper were charred, he remembered, and a gust of wind had lifted it from the smoking pile and dropped it at his feet. No one was looking, so he had picked it up and stuffed it in his pocket. A cartoon on the outside showed Negroes pursued by slave catchers; inside were some lines purported to have been written by an escaped slave: "He who had endured the pangs of slavery is the man to advocate liberty. Truth is of no color. God is the father of us all and we are brethren."

Reading in the privacy of his bedroom, James had felt rebuked by the voice of God Himself, commanding that he cast off the notion that slavery was good for the slave. And if it was not good for the slave, how could it be good for him, the master? He determined that he would accept no more unpaid labor from his servants. When he inquired discreetly about manumission, however, he discovered that giving freedom to a slave in these times of tumult was not only legally impossible but would cost him his church. The lawyer James had consulted admitted that abolition was the logical extension of the Declaration of Independence, but the system of slavery had been foisted on South Carolina and this was no time to talk of freeing the blacks.

That was in 1859. For several months James Hunnicutt did nothing. But he saw with sudden clearness the bitter determination of his parishioners to hold on to the slave system, come what may. It came to the point that Hunnicut could not look his own slaves in the eye. He would have to get them away to freedom.

He packed a few books and clothes and food for a long trip in a wagon one night and ordered the slave woman and the old man to the back of the canvas wagon. To Jeff—a man his own age—he handed the reins and climbed up beside him. It was not until they had been on the road for a week that he told his slaves his purpose. It took a month of riding together day after day before the barriers between master and slave broke down and Jeff and James Hunnicutt could talk together, man to man.

They were in Virginia by then and Jeff knew of a place in Fredericksburg—a station in the Underground Railroad. If they could be carried that far they'd be sent by the next trainload to Canada.

"Underground Railroad?"

Jeff explained. "It's not much good you take us North. Ain't nowhere safe for the colored since the law pass, Marsa."

How much the Negroes knew that the whites in the South hadn't dreamed of! He had never heard the Fugitive Slave

Law mentioned. James Hunnicutt had been ashamed at his ignorance and answered impatiently. "I asked you to stop calling me master." He had followed Jeff's advice and that was how, five years ago, he had come to Fredericksburg and met Lewis Lindsay, free Negro with an education surpassing his own and for years a stationmaster on the Underground, passing hundreds of fugitives across the border to freedom.

It was Lindsay who had persuaded the minister to stay in Virginia, take a church in Fredericksburg and try to get some sense into the heads of his white parishioners—for war, the Negro said, was inevitable as rain when the storm clouds were too heavy to carry their load of moisture.

Well, he had failed, James Hunnicutt said bitterly to himself. The slaveholders had learned nothing from his preaching or from four years of battle. They would accept the edict of emancipation for a time, but if and when they recovered their power they would restore slavery or something close to it.

Hunnicutt had done a lot of thinking, a lot of studying of American history, a lot of talking in secret to Lewis Lindsay and his friends. He had published a little religious journal, trying by moral persuasion and the precepts of the Bible to change the hearts of the whites. Now he was done with preaching. It was time for political action. He stepped briskly down from the pulpit and walked away from Fredericksburg on the day Abraham Lincoln was assassinated.

Lewis Lindsay was already in Richmond. That's where he would go.

"I have every hope that whites and Negroes may live together in harmony. But freedmen should not support white men who have opposed their liberty as delegates for the coming convention."

The speaker on the steps of the Richmond Courthouse was James Hunnicutt, editor of the *New Nation*. The time—early in May 1867. Two years had gone by since the guns of war had been silenced, but the states that had been in rebellion were still for the most part under military rule. The hope of immediate restoration of peaceful government envisioned by Lincoln had faded. It had become apparent that the men who had ruled the Confederacy were still determined on the white man's rule. But the four million freedmen who had won the right to take their place as American citizens were also determined. Even the most ignorant and bewildered among the former slaves knew that freedom was something more than relief from bodily cruelty and unpaid toil and having their children sold away from them—all that the former slaveholders were ready to concede. The great majority, Hunnicutt was sure, were aware of the meaning of the Declaration of Independence and the guarantees of the Constitution with its three new amendments. They knew as well as he did that the only way to protect their freedom was by taking part in governing the state. The Congress in Washington agreed. The Fourteenth Amendment passed last December stood witness. Many of their own race in the blue uniforms of the Federal Army were among the soldiers sent to protect their rights. Schoolteachers, Negro and white, had come from the North with the agents of the Freedmen's Bureau. But even with a few thousand newcomers in the state on their side, the Virginia Negroes were not numerous enough or strong enough in political experience to reorganize the state government without the votes and the leadership of some white Virginians.

This is why the hundred or so dark-skinned people around the Richmond Courthouse that May evening listened with enthusiasm to James Hunnicutt.

"Negroes who vote for rebels invite in perpetuity the whipping post, the chain gang and the vagrant laws. Anyone who refuses to sit in the coming Constitutional Convention with Negro delegates should not be supported for office."

Hunnicutt spoke plainly and they trusted him. For two years he had moved among them in friendship. Anybody was welcome at any time in the office of the newspaper he printed. A Negro ran his printing press, and Negro leaders like Dr. Thomas Bayne and Reverend Jessup wrote for his paper; Lewis Lindsay was his best friend. They called each other by their first names, but every other person of color Mr. Hunnicutt called Mr. or Mrs. A little thing, but not unimportant.

"Negroes should unite," the speaker continued, "to win the free schools, the decent wages, the land they need. . . ."

"Forty acres and a mule!" someone shouted.

Hunnicutt smiled and nodded. The need to distribute land to the landless was vital. So was justice in the courts, the right to be called for jury duty and to be accorded the common

Negro voters registered for the first municipal election to be held in Richmond, Virginia, since the end of the war.

courtesies as equal citizens under law. So much to be done and more to be undone!

"Negro workers are the bone and sinew of our state. Land, yes!" Hunnicut said. "And contracts for fair wages, education, the dignity due to American citizens. You won't get these things from the landed aristocracy, taught from childhood to believe every Negro inferior to every white man. Those people will have to be disfranchised. You must elect loyal congressmen, loyal governors."

"I guess we've made up our minds about a candidate for governor, Mr. Hunnicutt," Lewis Lindsay, in the front row, said meaningfully.

Cheers and cries of "Hunnicutt" came from the crowd. James Hunnicutt ignored the interruption.

"Before you think about electing officers, you've got to have a good constitution. At the Constitutional Convention next December, you've got to be there on the floor in person, as delegates. Negro voters and white workingmen's votes and the votes of those the Republican party have sent into Virginia, added together—"

"My boss calls them folks carpetbaggers." A young boy laughed.

"And I reckon he calls me a scalawag."

"Worse than that, Mr. Hunnicutt. He calls you a *radical* scalawag!"

"So we're all radicals." Hunnicutt joined in the laughter. "I am a white man. I do not desire to place black above white, but I do believe that whites and Negroes should be accorded exactly equal rights."

Meetings like this night after night drew bitter criticism from former slaveholders and murmured doubts from the moderates among the Republicans who claimed to hold principles of freedom but were afraid of going too far too fast. But Hunnicutt spoke from experience. He knew the thinking of slaveholders because he had been one himself and, almost alone among the Virginia leaders, knew the Negroes as companions and friends. He wanted what they wanted, what they had to have.

Through the summer and fall three factions struggled to gain ascendancy in the coming convention. The conservative newspapers suddenly printed editorials in praise of colored people who remained faithful to their masters' instruction. Hunnicutt warned in the *New Nation* that Negroes would do well to look with suspicion on ex-Confederates who all of a sudden praised where they had abused and ridiculed.

When flattery failed to entice the Negro voters, employers began to discharge Negroes who refused to register as Democrats. This tactic backfired because it drew the Freedmen's Bureau and Hunnicutt's followers closer together. But some within the Republican party continued to fear Hunnicutt and speak against him.

Then in November the conservatives had Hunnicutt arrested "for inciting the black to insurrection." This outraged the Negroes and frightened moderates such as Judge Underwood and Provisional Governor Welles, who knew very well that Hunnicutt had no such thought in mind. They got the military to intervene and he was released on bail "pending the outcome of the convention."

When December rolled around and the convention was called to order by Judge Underwood, James Hunnicutt was conceded to be the man of the hour. Of the 105 elected delegates, only thirty-three were from the former governing class and seventy-five were liberal reconstructionists. Of this group, twenty-five were Negroes and half as many more endorsed every section of Hunnicutt's program.

The Constitution, considered by competent historians to be "the only democratic instrument of government Virginia has ever had," was largely the handiwork of James Hunnicutt

and his Negro friends. Before ratification, the provisions dis-
barring all those who had supported secession were separated
from the body of the document and defeated.

"What are you looking so sad about, James?" Lewis Lindsay
asked his friend when the votes on ratification had been
counted. "We've won, 210,000 to 9,000!"

"We've won and we've lost," Hunnicutt answered sadly.

"Because the test oath was defeated? Some of our own
people thought it disbarred too many from voting."

"We could have made exceptions later as time went by.
Now those who opposed liberty all their lives will find ways
to destroy it. The whipping post and chain gang are gone.
The former slaveholders will vote them back. The Negroes
have free schools and the vote. Their schools will someday be
closed and the voting power whittled away. The Negro will
be crowded out. I ought to have found some way to prevent
it. Moral 'suasion, politics—nothing worked. I've failed you."

"We're not licked yet, Mr. Hunnicutt," Lewis Lindsay
answered. "And if we do run into trouble—well, we mean to
have our freedom. If we have it to do over again, I just hope
we have somebody around like you."

# Walk together, 7 children

The problems raised by the abolition of slavery and four years of civil war hung like a dark shadow over the Southern people, black and white, through the remainder of the nineteenth century. For the Negro Americans, the ten years of Reconstruction became only a sad, shining memory. The hope of one common freedom shared by high and low had been destroyed almost before it was born.

The total inferiority of the former slaves was not a myth to the majority of white Southerners. They believed it with fierce sincerity. They did not abandon their determination to rule the Southland and to keep it a "white man's country." While the scalawags and carpetbaggers and dark-skinned freedmen were grappling with the problems of government, powerful groups in the Deep South were organizing themselves into secret societies—the Knights of the Camelias, the Red Shirts, the Ku Klux Klan. With threats and ridicule they drove out the northern "carpetbaggers," those at least who had made the cause of Negro citizenship their own. The poor whites were drawn away from their Negro allies by flattery and welded together into one political party. The landed class, the businessmen, the propertyless, poorly paid working people —the aristocratic myth of white supremacy was stretched to include everyone with fair skin and straight hair. Then in 1876, having concluded a bargain with the North to withdraw the army and leave the problem of Negro citizenship in their "understanding" hands, they began isolating and disfranchising the freedmen.

The methods the Klansman used—the murders and lynchings and trickery—are no part of this story. The vain protests of a few white Southerners is. John Fee still persisted in teaching white and Negro students together at Berea College until in 1904 this was forbidden by law. And in New Orleans, the South's most famous novelist, George W. Cable, waged a bold though futile campaign in his book *The Silent South* to convince his fellow Southerners that "giving freedom to the slave" was in very truth the only way to give "freedom to the free."

Cable had been a Confederate soldier, the son of a small slaveholder. He wrote gently, temperately and well. But criticism of the rule of the white supremacist raised a storm. His books, articles and letters were called treasonable and a wanton insult to his "own people." In 1888 he gave up and moved to Massachusetts. Like the exiles of abolitionist days, Cable had to leave his home or keep silent, or stay, keep fighting and perhaps die.

One more try was made in 1896 by the few Negroes who still dared to go to the polls. For a brief moment they made common cause with white union workers and tenant farmers in a new political grouping, the Populist party. White leaders such as Tom Watson of Georgia raised high hopes that together they could win back the political power lost after Reconstruction. When their candidates failed to win, Watson blamed their failure on the unpopularity of the black man, smashed the alliance and became violently anti-Negro. Lynchings increased and Negro schoolhouses and churches were burned.

Once again the Negro was an alien in his own country, shut out behind an even higher wall of segregation. The most publicized spokesman he had—Booker T. Washington—preached submission and abandonment of the dream of full citizenship. Behind the Jim Crow wall, the sons and daughters of former slaves heard the words freedom and brotherhood only on Sunday in their churches, in the poetry of the Sermon on the Mount and in the hymns and "shouts" and sorrow songs of their ancestors—*"Woke up in the morning with my mind on freedom," "Go down Moses, set my people free,"* and *"Walk together, children."*

In the white part of town, other Christian men and women were hearing their preachers read the Sermon on the Mount too, but "the meek shall inherit the earth" had no connection in their minds with their cooks and gardeners. The wall between white and Negro Christians stood as strong and high on Sunday as on any other day of the week. There wasn't a black face in their minds when the minister preached "brotherhood."

Except for one spirited and courageous protest against lynching by Mrs. M. E. Tilley and a small group of churchwomen in 1912, no attempt was made by white Southerners to break down the barriers raised between those who should have been united. But in 1902 a ragged boy, the son of a part-time sharecropper, was growing up in the hill country of Tennessee. When he reached adulthood and entered the ministry, Reverend Claude Williams would sacrifice his livelihood and risk his life to remove a few bricks from the wall.

# Claude Williams

The two-room shack where Claude Williams was born perched at the top of fourteen arid acres of hilly land in west Tennessee. His father was part Cherokee Indian and proud of it, but that didn't make him more understanding about the plight of less fortunate Negroes down in the valley. Jess had come from the next county to marry Minnie Bell Galey, who had inherited the farm and slab house. She had never been more than ten miles from home in her life.

The farm didn't produce quite enough vegetables, hogs or chickens to feed the family. There were clothes to buy once in a while, and coffee and "sweetening" at the country store, besides tithing for the Cumberland Presbyterian Church. So the Williams family had to eke out their bare subsistence, sharecropping for a plantation owner in the fertile bottom lands a few miles south.

At the age of six Claude began earning his share of the hundred or two hundred dollars which was the family income. He was as ragged and underfed as the Negro boys who chopped cotton in the planter's fields on both sides of the

Williams' allotted plot; but he didn't have to live on the plantation as they did, and four months of the year he could go to school. He was glad to be free of the sight of black faces every night when they rode home behind the old mule. No Negroes lived in the hills, none of course went to the one-room school or to the white church for all-day worship on Sunday.

It had been his mother's ambition ever since he was born for Claude to become a preacher. But the boy, intensely religious, wasn't sure God wanted him. At fifteen he left home, to see what the world was like and to straighten things out in his own mind. For a year he lived with another farming family, the Stovers, and earned the money to pay his board by day labor on neighboring farms or on the railroad, or as a coal passer on the Mississippi River boat. When Fanny Stover heard Claude read passages from the Bible aloud with that golden voice of his, she said that he just had to be a preacher. The boy still doubted that he was worthy in the eyes of God.

Troubled, he enlisted in the Army. The year was 1916, and while he was in the service, World War I broke out—"the war to make the world safe for democracy." He was still in Officer's Training Camp in Minnesota when the Germans surrendered. He read and reread his Bible, still drawn to the religious life and torn with trying to make a decision. Another short hitch in the service and then he was offered a job in South America. Before leaving the country he made a trip home.

His mother had been praying for him in the isolated quiet of the Tennessee hills. After one month at home, Claude Williams was "one with God," studying in the Bible College at Bethel. The Cumberland Presbyterian school taught the narrow fundamentalist doctrines in which he had been raised. He hadn't thought of any other church.

At Bethel he met small, golden-haired Joyce King, studying to be a missionary. In the spring they were married, and

Claude always said that was the best thing that had happened to him in his whole life. When they had finished their schooling at Bethel, he entered the ministry under the more liberal U. S. A. Presbyterian synod at Auburntown, near Nashville. He preached six sermons every Sunday at the six small churches in his care and soon made a reputation as an orator and Bible scholar.

There was an old Negro who came every Sunday to one of his churches. He sat in the back, apart from the rest of the congregation. Claude couldn't help wondering about the old man sitting there, Sunday after Sunday, listening as if he understood the sermon. One Sunday, when Claude was standing at the door to shake hands with his parishioners, he impulsively stretched out his hand to the Negro.

The other whites standing nearby were plainly startled, and he felt odd himself with his hand in a black hand. But did not Jesus preach brotherhood and were we not all God's children, black and white alike? It was a new thought to the earnest young preacher.

There were a great many Negroes in the area around Auburntown, living a life totally separate from the community, except to serve it as laborers or house servants. They had a rickety church—an old schoolhouse that had been abandoned because the roof was falling in. Claude went down there one Sunday, after all his other preaching was done, to preach to the colored folk, and was stirred by the devoutness of the congregation gathered in the decrepit building. Some white people had heard that he was coming and were settled in the best seats, obviously amused to hear their minister preaching the word of God to ignorant, primitive blacks.

Claude Williams looked at the complacent, well-dressed whites seated on one side and the colored women with babies in their laps and the men in overalls on the other. He looked at the sagging roof with the night stars shining through and he put two dollars in the collection basket and made sure that the visitors did the same. When he witnessed the gratitude of the colored congregation and knew that they would be able to repair their church, he felt ashamed. Suddenly he knew that there was more to religion, more to life, than he'd been taught at Bethel, or in the Army either.

He had heard of some summer courses that would be given in Nashville and arranged to go there to learn more. The lectures and reading under the very liberal scholar, Dr. Alva Taylor, opened his mind to a new world. He found other young Southerners in the school as puzzled about things as he was, "hungering for release through knowledge" as he afterward put it to Joyce, "for release from the prison of bigotry and superstition."

Alva Taylor saw the teaching of Jesus and the Hebrew prophets as part of a great age-long search for human understanding of the universe. He compared their message with that of other great spiritual teachers, Lao-Tzu and Buddha, and with the new discoveries in physics and geology and biology. Religion, he said, was not just a way for a person to gain a seat in heaven, but a program for action in the America of their own day.

It was a wonderful experience for young men listening to him, but Claude went home troubled. He could no longer preach the thundering sermons about Satan that his congregations loved to hear. He saw now that Satan tempted, not with dancing and cards and smoking and drinking, but by letting people exploit the poor and the oppressed, black as well as white. He couldn't even preach that the elect of God's earth were limited to one sect—U. S. A. Presbyterians. He thought he'd have to leave the ministry.

"I can't be a preacher without being a hypocrite," he said to Joyce. But she saw a way. "Preach what you believe," she answered.

The next spring Claude went back to study under Dr. Taylor and came away with an understanding of Southern history different from the way he'd learned it in school. He and his friends met and discussed things with students at Fisk, the Negro college at Nashville.

"I'm ready in my *mind* to act as if skin color does not matter," Claude said to Howard Kester, another young Southerner, "but I was brought up to be prejudiced."

"So was I," Kester admitted.

They decided to try out their new theories of equality at a summer camp in Mississippi being conducted by the Fellowship of Conciliation, an organization from the North. At the camp Claude sat at the same table with Negroes, slept in the same dormitory. For the first time he heard himself calling Negroes, "Mr." and "Mrs." and by their last names. After a couple of days he began to feel at ease as all the group played together, sang together. He was proud to write Joyce that he had made some Negro friends. Before the week was up he forgot who was white and who was dark-skinned. They were just people. And he knew that he had preached brotherhood but had never practiced it in his life before.

He tried to share his experience with his congregation when he got back to Auburntown, but even his warmest admirers thought he had gone crazy. "He wants us to sit down and eat at the same table with 'em."

Claude and Joyce knew that he couldn't preach in Auburntown much longer. The Presbyterian Home Mission Synod offered him a church with only twenty members in Paris, Arkansas. It was a coal-mining center, the head of the synod explained, but there were plantations in the bottom land near the Arkansas River bank. In the run-down cabins on the plantations lived about two hundred Negroes, starvation poor and without a school or church, but being colored of course they weren't welcome up on the hill. He didn't know what

Claude could do in this unpromising community, but Paris needed a man like him.

The salary would be $1800, just half of what he'd been making. Part would be paid by the congregation, part by the Board of Missions. It was not much for a man and wife and two children, but Joyce said that they could get by. The people in Auburntown couldn't understand why a brilliant young man would want to step down in the world. "If you'd drop all this nonsense about colored people," one of them said, "our best pulpits would be open to you. You could make $10,000 a year, in time."

The landscape in Arkansas was like the Tennessee hill country, sharecropper cabins and fields of cotton, sycamore trees and willow. Pretty, except right near Paris where the coal mines began . . . Black gashes in the hills and straight rows of little houses too close together, the "company towns" owned by the people who owned the mines. Joyce and Claude drove into the center of town in their secondhand truck, with the furniture and books and household goods and the two little girls piled in the back. Claude pulled up at the "manse," next to the church and felt, before he'd ever lived there, that he was coming home.

Paris wasn't much of a place—no parks, no library, no place for young people to go except a pool hall. Claude soon learned that no young people set foot in his church. For the first two weeks he preached to exactly twenty people, all past middle age, all "leaders" in the community, leaders without followers. The young people and the blacksmith, the barber, the miners and their families stayed away.

Claude ordered a pool table and other games and fixed up an unused wing of the church, with a corner for books and pictures of Jesus and Jefferson and Eugene Debs on the wall, and invited the high school students to come whenever they liked. He invited the miners, too. The young people were a little cagey at first, but the preacher and his wife were like-able people, and they told one another he didn't carry his preaching outside the pulpit. Soon, from the close of school until dark, the church recreation room was crowded with boys and girls and, after suppertime every night, with the men from the mines.

The church members didn't say anything. The Board of Missions, which was paying half the minister's salary, had promised Claude a free hand. His sermons at morning worship were straight from the Bible, and his Sunday evening talks, in which he told familiar Bible stories with sometimes a word about how they could be applied right here in Paris, were so interesting that young people came drifting in from the recreation room to listen.

An occasional miner might be seen standing in the back, near the door. (They didn't have any clothes except their grimy work clothes, not 'fitten,' they said, for church.)

The blacksmith, the barber, the clerk from the general store who belonged to another church began coming to the Sunday evening meetings and borrowing the books Claude talked about.

Claude had lost no time in visiting with the black families in the bottoms. He found them at first rather reticent and suspicious of a white man who had come neither to sell anything nor to spy. But his warm smile was disarming and his clothes were shabby enough to make them feel comfortable. After a while they felt enough at home with him to share both their jokes and their problems. The door of the manse was always open to them—the *front* door. If it was mealtime they were invited to draw up to the table, and they noticed that Mrs. Williams didn't even pull down the shades.

Claude had started a small revolution in Paris, Arkansas.

When the miner's union went out on strike for better wages and safety measures in the mines, Claude spoke publicly in church in favor of the strike.

There was great poverty among the miners, almost as much as among the Negro sharecroppers. Very few had more than a third-grade education. He wrote letters for them and prepared their resolutions to send back to the national office.

Neither the miners nor the Negro sharecroppers belonged to his church but they were—it seemed to him—part of his flock just the same.

The strike settlement did not give the miners all they asked for but a little more than they had had before. They were grateful for Claude's help and made him a member of their union. He carried his card with pride.

At about this same time, the young people in Paris decided that they wanted to hold a public dance at graduation. The principal of the high school and most of the parents belonged to churches opposed to dancing. Dancing, according to these adults, was sinful, and a public dance out of the question. Claude preached a sermon on the natural need of human beings to play, to sing, to express their joy in life through rhythm. That didn't convince anybody, so he and Joyce got some gramophone records and held a *private* dance in the recreation room of the church. This was too much for the staid church members.

While the people of Paris debated the morality of dancing, the rest of the country reeled under the impact of the stock market crash. The market plummeted in October 1929, but it wasn't until after Christmas that Paris, Arkansas, began to feel the effects. The mines closed. Cotton prices dropped. The economy of the town ground to a slow stop. The shortage of money was bad enough, but the idleness—no work day after day—was even harder to cope with.

Claude Williams came up with two plans to relieve the

situation. Funds must be raised to get food and clothing for the destitute—for the children here in town and for the Negro children of the sharecroppers down by the river. The man who owned the moving-picture show would open the show on a Sunday afternoon and give all the proceeds to start the fund. Movies on Sunday? In Paris, Arkansas? The ministers of the other churches, the Baptists and Methodists and Camp-bellites, united in drawing up a petition against the immorality of showing movies on Sunday. It seemed to them as sinful as dancing, though they knew that the wealthier people often drove to Fort Smith, the nearby city, where the moving-picture theaters were open on Sunday. The wealthy people were already angry at Claude Williams for his support of the miners' union. This was a chance to protest the changes he was bringing to the town. They signed the "four-square" church petitions. But Claude went ahead anyhow, held the moving-picture show, raised the needed money.

The second part of his plan was more important. Sometimes in after years Claude thought it the most important thing he had ever done. He proposed that the workers—Negro and white, employed and unemployed—use their idle time to build a great Temple of Labor on the half-acre lot adjoining the church. They'd quarry stone for the walls of the temple from the hills and they'd call it the Proletarian Church and Labor Temple. He explained that "proletarian" to his mind simply meant all those who worked with their hands. Union meetings could be held in the temple, and there'd be room for a gymnasium and a printing press for their own kind of newspaper.

The idea struck a spark. An architect who hadn't had any work for months drew the plans—without pay. A small businessman offered free sand and gravel. Miners, farmers, carpenters, stonemasons pledged free labor. Only one necessary ingredient was lacking and that was cement for the foundation. Claude cashed in his life insurance policy to buy the cement. The church fathers did not object to the land being used. Their property was being improved at no expense to the church.

On the lot a huge wooden cross was set up with a banner bearing the words, *That They Might Have Life More Abundantly.*

The town people and the sharecroppers went at the project with a fierce enthusiasm, digging, quarrying, hauling. While the dream of the Temple of Labor was still no more than a huge hole in the ground, the national head of the Board of Missions wrote "I am astonished at Williams. I hope he will live through it. It is a daring and radical thing to do—what we all desire to do sometime in our ministry. It is delightful to see how his own church and the working classes are helping him. He has some of the breath-taking courage that the greatest Christians have had in their difficult measures."

*Life more abundantly* . . . As the Depression deepened it had become a question in the Arkansas backwoods whether the poor people could hold life together at all. The stone foundation of the temple stood with the cross and banner, because there was simply no money anywhere for the materials needed by the workers to go ahead with the building.

Claude Williams was appointed one of three commissioners to investigate and report on conditions in that area so the Federal government—Franklin D. Roosevelt's New Deal government—could plan what measures to take. But appetite and sickness and cold and despair cannot wait on long-term planning and wrangling in Congress. The suffering that Claude saw in his investigations was beyond bearing. He had only one remedy—to organize the unemployed into a union so they could speak for themselves.

Workers' Alliances were coming into existence in various parts of the country. But except for the locals of the United

Mine Workers there was scarcely a union in Arkansas. Claude spoke to groups of sharecroppers, white and black. The Negroes had been so mistreated that they were suspicious of whites, even those in the same desperate condition as themselves. But they trusted the preacher and were willing to form the new union. It was a tougher job convincing the whites. Unite with Negroes? They had all the built-in prejudices inherited from days of slavery. But both groups believed in Claude Williams, in his wisdom and sincerity. Little by little they began to accept the idea of racial cooperation.

Joyce worried about her husband's health; she worried about the unfinished Temple of Labor that had been Claude's dream. She worried, too, though she never said so, about the half of his salary that was supposed to be paid by the congregation. It had been stopped once before but now it was cut off entirely. The church members felt threatened as they saw the separation between white and black begin to weaken. Nor did they like the many new members from among the miners coming into their church.

Claude was aware of their disapproval but was too busy to do anything about it. It was no surprise to get a copy of a petition signed by eleven church members asking a hearing by the presbytery "to study the conditions and if it seem wise to the presbytery to dissolve the existing pastoral relationship between the Reverend Claude Williams and the Presbyterian Church of Paris."

Within a month Claude was officially removed from his church "for the good of the Kingdom of God." A few days later he received formal notice to vacate the manse. Without his pastorate his family had neither a roof over their heads nor the $900 salary paid by the Board of Missions. And there was the Temple of Labor still unbuilt. He decided to appeal the decision of the local presbytery. It was useless. An ex-Confederate colonel put the matter plainly: "The preacher is against good government. Right or wrong, the Negroes will never have social equality in the South."

Paris was no longer Claude Williams' parish. The truck was loaded once again with their household luggage and the children perched on top of the load. They went first to Fort Smith, then to Little Rock, fighting always the battle of the poor and oppressed. They had no money at all except what people gave them. It didn't occur to Claude that they were worse off than the sharecroppers they were trying to help. In Little Rock he led a great hunger march of unemployed (whites, Negroes, Mexicans and Indians) to the capital. He was arrested and thrown into jail. Another time he was pulled out of his car and beaten. Nothing stopped him in the work he felt called on to do.

Two years after his departure from Paris, Claude Williams was back again for a weekend conference of the State Federation of Labor. He stood a long time staring at the sturdy foundations of the never-to-be-built temple, as if he were seeing in reality the inscription he had meant to have over the doorway: *That They Might Have Life More Abundantly.* The banner was gone and tufts of grass were pushing up through cracks in the cement. It occurred to him that the rough blades of grass were like the prejudices still dividing the peoples of America. Would the foundations for the beautiful country America could be—would they last? Would the walls ever rise?

The Temple of Labor was never finished. Claude never got back to Paris, Arkansas, but in 1938 he was wandering through Alabama and heard about the interracial Conference for Human Welfare. He made his way to Birmingham and sat there in that huge audience of white and dark-skinned Southerners, and it was as if his own banner were flying from that platform: *That They Might Have Life More Abundantly.*

Claude Williams has never stopped dreaming and working for the fulfillment of his dreams. He is an old man now but a free spirit still working with others when he finds them going his way—alone in a small home in south Alabama, preaching, writing, helping in the Freedom Movement.

# Common
# 8 ground

"Negroes don't know whites, and whites don't know Negroes,"
Louis Lomax, Negro journalist commented in 1962. Although
a few rare individuals like Claude Williams had made an effort to bridge the chasm, Negroes and whites in the South
couldn't visit each other in their homes. They could not stop
to visit on the street, or go to a concert together, or take books
from the same library without challenging the overwhelming
sentiment of the community in which they had to live. Unless
they were ready to become outcasts, white Southerners had
to be very circumspect. For a Negro to cross the color barrier
could mean death.

In the 1930s a few white Southern writers began to use
words as weapons and to speak out about conditions in the
South. But novels such as those by DuBose Heyward, William Faulkner and Lillian Smith, fictional stories laid in the
South they knew, with Negro characters drawn as human
beings and not as comic stereotypes, were read by few
Southerners. Such works as *Strange Fruit* by Lillian Smith
were deeply resented. The works of Negro writers such as
W. E. B. Du Bois, James Weldon Johnson, Langston Hughes
and Richard Wright were ignored.

In the Southern universities a few sociologists spoke out
against lynching and Jim Crow. They usually lost their jobs.
Two young scholars who published revealing studies of conditions in the Southern states met with such bitter criticism

that they committed suicide. A few young men such as Don West and John Beecher published slim volumes of poetry.

Books and individual protests were immensely valuable, but they did not provide a means of communication between Negro Americans and white Americans such as would create a common ground for action. More fruitful in these years were the events taking place in Washington. Franklin Roosevelt had gathered around him in the various agencies of the government many thoughtful white Southerners such as Aubrey Williams, Clifford Durr and his wife from Alabama, Clark Foreman from Georgia, who worked closely with the Administration. Claude Pepper represented Florida in the Congress and Justice Hugo Black of Alabama left the Senate for the Supreme Court.

Negro leaders were called to the capital specifically as advisers on Negro affairs. Some of these—such as Robert Weaver and Ralph Bunche—were not Southerners; but Mrs. Mary Church Terrell, William Trent, young John Killens and grand old Mrs. Mary McLeod Bethune were Southern, "born and raised." Between these Southern whites and Negroes in Washington enduring friendships were formed.

Yet in the South itself there was no way that members of the two races could come together to seek a common ground of action. The isolation was so complete that a Northern journalist, reporting on a journey through the Southern states, wrote that he had found only one Southerner really concerned about civil rights for the Negro people—a young professor at the University of Alabama by the name of Joseph Gelders. Joe was neither pleased nor flattered at this comment. "If I thought that was true," he said, "I'd quit trying. There are hundreds of us." It was important to him that Negroes realize that they were not alone in their struggle; but it was not until three years later, in 1938, that Joe had an opportunity to do something about the problem.

He had resigned from the university and was in Birming-

The Conference for Human Welfare called for an end to discrimination and segregation in 1938—the same demands made at the close of the Civil War!

ham, his home, working for a Northern-based committee to bring a greater measure of justice for Negroes in the courts and to defend their right to join the CIO industrial unions being organized in the mines and steel mills. The CIO unions accepted members without discrimination, and Negro miners and steel workers had some opportunity to meet with white labor on the basis of equality. But mineowners, the steel companies and the city government alike bitterly opposed the establishment of a strong union in the area, especially a union that admitted Negro workers into its ranks.

Joe Gelders and others did what they could to defend the workers and those who were organizing them. One night on his way from a meeting, Joe was waylaid and beaten and left for dead on a country road. He recovered from the attack and, more determined than ever, set out to find a way in which Negroes and sympathetic white Southerners could work together and plan for a change of conditions.

With the strong support of Mrs. Roosevelt, two hundred sponsors, Negro and white, were enlisted from all over the South for a Conference for Human Welfare. The interracial conference was held in Birmingham, Alabama, in November 1938. Twelve hundred people answered the call to this all-inclusive meeting of Southerners, "white and black together."

A program was adopted which included a call for "full democracy for all people regardless of color; full civil rights and an end to discrimination and segregation"—the same demands made by the Negroes seventy-two years before, at the end of the Civil War! Those who attended the conference saw it as a new beginning—a seedbed from which a rich harvest would be gathered.

Southwide conferences were held every year for the next six years and provided a base for continuing work. World War II interrupted the yearly meetings, but left the important branch, the Southern Educational Conference Fund under Jim

Dombrowski intact. *The Southern Patriot,* the monthly journal published by the Educational Conference is today for whites and Negroes one of the most influential organs the modern liberation movement possesses.

But small committees and yearly conferences, no matter how heartening, did not solve the problem. The wall still stood with its dividing signs: *White* and *Colored.* What was needed was a meeting place for the day-by-day contact necessary for real communication. Myles Horton, who had attended that first Conference for Human Welfare in Birmingham, provided such a meeting place at the Highlander Folk School, high on the mountains at Monteagle, Tennessee.

# Myles
# Horton

Myles Horton, tall and lean with a Southern drawl to his speech and a back-country, perpetual sunburn, could pose for the portrait of his ancestor who, the records say, came across the Cumberland mountains with three other explorers and an eighteen-year-old slave called Jamie in 1766.

Myles was born in 1905, a year that saw the Southern legislatures scrambling to pass laws fastening Jim Crow customs firmly into the body politic of the Southern states. His boyhood was spent in the rural village of Savannah, Tennessee, about one hundred miles from Memphis. From there he went to college at Cumberland University, an all-white school. From Cumberland he went to Union Theological Seminary for a year and to Chicago the next year for graduate study in sociology. In both places Myles encountered deep interest in the rising concept of Christianity to be *lived* rather than merely prayed for. The concern of the young theological students was for social justice, for the rights of workers to form unions, for relief of the abysmal poverty among the unemployed, especially the Negroes and the mountain whites in the South. Of the daily lives of the Negroes, of their history, Myles Horton knew little.

Myles knew all about the mountain whites. His mother and his aunt had always been interested in the "uplift" of these not so distant neighbors, many of whose ancestors had pioneering backgrounds like their own.

He became fired with the possibilities of the adult education programs started here and there in the Southern mountains. The folk school movement was international, its center in the Scandinavian countries. When Myles had an opportunity to go to Denmark for study, he jumped at it. He stayed abroad a year, learned Danish, lectured in that language at several of the folk schools and published enthusiastic articles in various magazines. When he came home, he knew what he wanted to do but he had no idea how to begin without financial resources. The country was in the midst of a deepening economic depression.

He himself had no money at all. The family had never had much, nor been concerned with money as such or with getting ahead in the world. His father had been dead for some time and his mother "managed."

Somebody he talked to at the University of Tennessee mentioned a Dr. Lillian Johnson, a teacher from Memphis who had taught for a long time at the university. She had ideas about Negroes and whites needing to come closer to-gether.

Miss Johnson was pretty old, they said, and had retired to a farm she'd bought in the village of Monteagle, right in the mountains. There weren't any colored people living there, but some lived in the same county at the foot of the mountain in Pelham. When Dr. Johnson heard there wasn't any school for Negroes in the whole of Grundy County, she got herself elected to the school board and gave the land and building for an elementary school, a one-room school with a single teacher. It was rumored that when the colored teacher drove over the mountain to the county seat every month to get her pay, she stopped and visited with Dr. Johnson and they sometimes sat and had tea or lemonade together. Her neighbors didn't like this much, but Dr. Johnson did a lot of nice things for them so they didn't complain. Myles decided he'd go to see this old lady.

The area Myles walked through was not a ghost town but a ghost country, beautiful and serene with sycamores and sweet gum trees and great clumps of wild rhododendron in bloom, magnificent in every way, until you came to a cabin in a clearing. The houses were weather-beaten, unpainted, with cardboard instead of glass in the windows and sagging piazzas where the barefoot owners sat with their hands hang-ing listless, their eyes staring ahead at nothing, having nothing, expecting nothing better than what they had. This was poverty and hopelessness such as Myles had rarely seen.

Doggedly he went on with that long, loose stride of his until he came to the Johnson farmhouse high on the brow of the hill. The young man and the old woman took to each other at once. Scarcely stopping for an introduction, they plunged into a discussion of their hopes and ambitions. Myles had a plan and no money to carry it out.

"Negroes don't know whites; whites don't know Negroes.

There isn't any meeting place anywhere where barriers could be broken down." What he had in mind was a folk school. Not one that taught just the rudiments of reading and writing, important as they were, but a folk school that taught brotherhood, where people of both races could live for a week or two at a time, eat together, sleep under the same roof. And something more. Meeting in the quiet leisure of the country, they could lay plans for action to take back to their own communities.

"And the mountain people? The neighbors?" Dr. Johnson asked quietly when the talk had run far into the night.

"The neighbors. Of course. They could be a part of it, as far as they were willing. A school such as that would bring the mountain people out of their isolation," Myles urged.

It sounded good. Dr. Johnson had taught enough young men and women at the university to judge the quality of the man staring down at her from his stand by the fireplace. She had no family of her own and had been wondering for a long time what would happen to the place she had built up when she was gone. Now on the strength of one night's conversation she made up her mind. The hopes and ambitions of this young stranger paralleled her own. *To be useful and used . . .*

She offered him the house and spacious land for a year to try out his program. Then if it worked, she would give him the place for his school. She had a little house in Knoxville, near the university, she said. She might stay there or she might travel. "When you're old," she added, as if he were doing her a favor, "you get in a hurry to do so many things."

"I've got some friends who might come to help," he said. "And there's my mother and Zilphia. [Zilphia was his wife.] I'd like it if you'd stay too."

Lillian Johnson shook her head. "Just long enough to get you acquainted. Mae Justus in the cottage down the brow of the hill will be a help to you. She's a writer. And there's the Marlowes and Matty Church—dear, good, sweet people. But they'll look at you with suspicion for your integration ideas. They do at me for days after Mrs. Kennedy, the schoolteacher, stops in. They can't help thinking the way they do— it's been pounded into all of us so long. As if God would make one people to be *inferior!* Maybe when they see your school . . . Anyway, you build your program for a year."

It was hard going the first year of the Highlander Folk School with less than one hundred dollars a month to spend.

Monteagle in the mountains was quieter than most places. There was no mounting unemployment, for nobody had had work for years, not since the local mine closed down. No bank mortgages were foreclosed because no bank would loan on the miserable shacks. People who had nothing could lose nothing. They were just a little closer to starvation than before.

Zilphia Horton shared the potatoes, beans and garden vegetables they had, carrying little bags of food from house to house. With her capacity for making friends, she removed much of the distrust mountain people had for strangers.

It caused no stir in the neighborhood when two young theological seminary graduates, Jim Dombrowski and Don West, brought a group of unemployed miners to work out plans for improving their existence. Among them were a couple of Negroes. They had worked in the mines with the others but had lived quite apart. In the weeks at Highlander, discussing plans for organizing a union, everybody ate at the table together, shared the same makeshift sleeping quarters; in short, they were *people* together.

Money continued to be a problem. Myles drew no salary, only his food and lodging and an occasional suit of clothes to look presentable when he went around the country explaining about the school and raising money to cover its expenses. When the people who came to study were able, they paid their expenses; but many could not afford even the nominal fee, so he collected money for scholarships. He didn't own the school, even after Dr. Johnson turned over the property for his permanent use. The charter he took out in 1934 to run a school was in the name of a cooperative group of interested friends. This informal arrangement was to make difficulties in the end, but that was the way Highlander was planned and the way it was run for thirty years.

Over the years about two Residential Adult Workshops a month were scheduled, with an average attendance of fifty or sixty people. Being at Highlander meant having the experience of living together, sharing, on the quiet mountaintop, a common goal. For hundreds of people of both races, barriers were broken down. Joe Gelders and Jim Dombrowski, before and after he became director of the Southern Educational Conference, were frequent visitors. Guy Carawan, the folk singer, made his home at Highlander; Mrs. Rosa Parks, before her historic refusal to give up her seat on the Montgomery bus, and Martin Luther King, Jr., attended workshops.

Myles found himself in the later years relying more and more on the practical wisdom of the Southern Negroes, people like Mrs. Septima Clark of Charleston and Esau Jenkins, the almost illiterate but very wise bus driver from a little island off the South Carolina coast. It was from Esau Jenkins that the idea of the "Citizenship Schools" came to life.

In 1955 Mrs. Clark brought Esau Jenkins with her to Highlander for a second time. The week's discussion had been devoted to trying to find ways to support the United Nations. "Before the people on Jones Island are in any position to do anything for the United Nations," Esau Jenkins said bluntly, "they need a school to teach them to read so they can register to vote in their own state."

The Citizenship Schools had their start on Jones Island a few months later. Myles and Zilphia went to Charleston to

Rosa Parks, who was arrested in 1955 for sitting in a bus in front of white passengers, was a frequent visitor to Highlander.

help Esau and Mrs. Septima Clark set up the first one. (This was the last trip Myles and Zilphia took together, for a few months later she died.)

The Citizenship School was no sooner under way than Septima Clark was informed that her teaching contract in Charleston would not be renewed. When Myles heard the news he wrote at once, asking Mrs. Clark to become Director of Workshops and Education for Highlander. The bus boycott was going on in Montgomery. More than two years had gone by since the Supreme Court had outlawed segregation

in the public schools, and not a school board in the Deep South had agreed to obey the law of the land.

Myles and Septima kept plugging away at the development of Citizenship Schools to make new voters of citizens who had waited so long. The Southern white supremacists in the Federal Congress saw in voter-registration drives of this type the greatest threat to their power. Agents of various Federal agencies and committees came to Grundy County to see what was going on. Their presence and the activities of segregationists from the Tennessee legislature stirred up old fears among the neighbors against the integrated Highlander School. The "snoopers" managed to get the country store to refuse to sell cigarettes or Cokes or candy to the Negro visitors, and there was less friendliness than before and some mild grumbling.

Myles was not too much disturbed. The local authorities had tried several times to revoke the school charter. He went right ahead with his program of "combatting intolerance and promoting understanding between rural and urban people and between members of all races, creeds, and complexions."

In the spring of 1959 Myles was invited to go to Europe as American representative of the International Adult Education Association. A busy schedule was planned for the summer session at Highlander, but nothing Mrs. Clark and the rest of the staff could not handle. He went off with an easy mind.

On July 31, the last night of a week's workshop, there'd been the usual closing banquet. The fifty or so guests were still seated at long board tables in the assembly hall waiting while Septima Clark set up the movie screen to show a documentary, *The Face of the South,* when the district attorney arrived with a search warrant.

Mrs. Clark and three of the guests who dared question the legality of the raid were taken to jail. The original charge by which Septima Clark was brought before the justice of the peace was "operating a nuisance." The district attorney admitted that this was just an excuse. The real purpose was to close the school and revoke its charter because it was conducting an institution in opposition to the segregation laws of the state of Tennessee.

The verdict of guilty in the local court was immediately appealed. Mrs. Clark and the others were out on bail and the school was running with more than usual enthusiasm when Myles came home. He was determined to fight the case in the courts and in the meantime continued to hold more workshops, which had larger attendances than ever before.

Myles Horton testifies before a committee investigating the activities of the Highlander School.

"While our program goes ahead unimpeded," he said, "friends around the country are defending our right to educate for democracy."

All this was true, but he had to admit to himself that the segregationists were going to destroy the school if there was any way under law to do it. As a precaution, the all-important Citizenship Schools were transferred in 1961 to a cooperative community center in McIntosh, Georgia. The Residential Workshops, the wonderful experimental interracial living, continued at the house on the mountain until the decision of the United States Supreme Court was handed down early in 1962. The judges decided that they could not review the findings of the Tennessee courts since there were no constitutional questions involved.

Highlander's charter was revoked, the buildings and land

that meant so much to so many Southern people were confiscated by the state on a legal technicality which Myles refused to waste further time contesting.

"Highlander was never simply real estate with buildings on it," he said. "Highlander was and is an idea. And who can kill an idea by confiscating it and attempting to smother it? While buildings can't be moved, an idea remains alive anywhere and everywhere in the hearts of men and women who believe in it enough to fight for it." On the same day that the state of Tennessee took possession of the Monteagle property he applied for and received a new charter for the Highlander Center for Research and Education in the city of Knoxville.

Understandably he felt a personal sorrow. "There is no use ignoring the fact that those of us on the Highlander staff and all friends of Highlander are deeply moved. The rolling hills, the nearby woods, our little lake . . . have created emotional associations not easy to relinquish."

Myles Horton was not a Grimké forced into exile in order to speak. He was not driven out of a church as Claude Williams had been, not, like so many others, deprived of a job. He was never in physical danger, never jailed or beaten. Or, like John Fairfield, killed.

Neither has he been frightened into silence. The new Highlander has suffered constant harassment, it is true. The summer camp near Knoxville was burned to the ground. A bomb thrown through a window in the Knoxville headquarters did great damage. But the new Highlander, like the old, stands ready to fight for the right of all people, whatever their race, religion or political persuasion, to meet together on the common ground of democracy.

# A house
# 9 to live in

Freedom of speech, freedom of religion, freedom from fear, freedom from want: President Roosevelt's four freedoms, blazoned on the walls of every USO hut from Samoa to Berlin, were taken as a promise by the soldiers in World War II. In the Battle of the Bulge, just before Germany surrendered, whites and Negroes fought side by side in the same units. A white sergeant from South Carolina had objected. After the battle he said, "When I saw how the colored soldiers fought, I changed my mind. They're just like any other soldiers now to me." A Virginian agreed. "The only trouble was getting them to stop. I have every respect for those men."

Respect and to be treated as men! This is all Negro Americans had been wanting for three hundred years. The veterans had come home expecting things to be different.

It hadn't happened. The segregationists in the Southern states and their representatives in the Federal government gave the military command: "As you were."

In the North and West, even with the ending of the Fair Employment Practices Committee, conditions had improved in employment and in the acceptance of a few Negro families as an integral part of community life. However, everywhere, finding a decent house to live in remained an acute problem. The question of "open housing"—that is, the right of anyone without regard to color or race, anyone at all who had the money to pay for it, to buy a house of his choice—became a burning problem. With the power of the ballot, with the help of legal decisions in the courts and sympathetic public opinion on their side, it was possible for the Negro people to believe that this battle, too, could be won.

However the question arose, "Where does the South begin, where does it end?" How far does the wall of segregation extend?

In the border state of Kentucky, in the 1950s, a young white couple, the Bradens, and a determined young Negro veteran put the question to the test as they reached out their hands to one another and tried to make a breach in the wall.

# Anne
# Braden

In 1939 a teen-age girl won the high school oratorical contest in the city of Anniston, Alabama, with a recitation of the Bill of Rights. She had enjoyed memorizing the sonorous phrases. The words of the First Amendment, especially, gave her a wonderful feeling being a part of this America, with the right to speak and think and worship as she pleased. Her mother and father were present to see her get the prize, and she knew they were proud of her. The president of the Civic Club that had arranged the contest was also pleased that Anne had won. She was the daughter of one of the "best" families of Anniston, an attractive young girl and a credit to the town.

Anne and her parents drove home through the sweet-smelling spring night. As they passed the gray stone Episcopal Church where she went every Sunday, for some reason part of the church ritual came to Anne's mind: *Oh God, who hast made of one blood all nations of men to swell on the face of the whole earth . . .* It seemed to her that the Bill of Rights she had memorized included not just people like themselves but all mankind, even Negroes on the other side of town.

Thoughts like these had been the fabric of her daydreaming lately. She was a great reader, in love with words, and somehow a lot of the best things she read about freedom and brotherhood stirred up questions about the colored people. She didn't talk about it because her mother would just say, as she always did, that there wasn't any reason to feel sorry for the colored people. They were perfectly happy and contented, with nothing to worry about because they had good Southern white people to take care of them. It was regrettable, she sometimes added, that they had ever been brought from Africa in the first place, but that was the fault of Northern shipowners and had happened a long time ago. There was nothing to do about it—and they did make good servants. So Anne kept her thoughts to herself.

Her father stopped the car at the brown, two-story house that had been "home" ever since the family moved to Anniston when Anne was seven years old. It was comfortable, but not imposing like the newer places being built above the country club on the side of the mountain.

They were not wealthy. The father was just a salesman for a big firm, not a mill owner or a lawyer or a judge like most of his friends. They had something better than wealth to assure them a place in the elite society of the north Alabama town—Anne's mother came from one of the oldest families of Kentucky. Her great-grandfather had been lieutenant governor of that state before the Civil War.

Being from an old family brought moral obligations of course. Anne's mother was always very kind to the poor whites across the tracks who worked in the mills. She sewed for the foreign missions at the church. And never, or hardly ever, turned away a beggar from the back door. She was undemanding and polite to her Negro servants and had explained once to Anne, "It's not only a Christian way to act, but if you're good to them, they're faithful." She never said "nigger" but always "colored" when talking about them. But when Anne was eight or nine her mother had to correct her on one occasion. Anne had spoken of the washwoman as a "colored lady."

"You never call colored people ladies," she explained. "You say 'colored woman' and 'white lady.'"

There were many little niceties of that kind that a Southern mother had to explain to her children in order to keep race relations as they should be. Not as many for the white as for the Negro mother of course, and it was not as serious if their children made a mistake. Still, Anne had never heard anybody question segregation; she had never questioned it herself. But there *were* things she minded. A shiver always ran through her when a rumor went around that there had been another lynching. So when she heard, during that summer after school was out, that Congress was talking about passing an anti-lynch law, she was glad.

One day at the library she met an old friend of her father's and spoke of the bill. He was dead against it and in the course of the discussion said something that jolted her. "You have to have a good lynching once in a while," he said in his gentle, courtly manner, "so that Nigra will know his place."

This was what came of segregation! It was a poison, a sickness that could make a kind old man say a horrible thing like that. She walked out of the library, too upset to choose a book.

She didn't mention to her father anything about having talked to his friend. She was afraid to. What if he, too . . ? She was very close to her indulgent father, pleased at his pride about her good grades at school, pleased with his outgoing generosity. Once she had seen him slip money to Mattie, the cook, to pay her house rent when he found out she was running short.

He talked to Anne about her future, seemed glad when she decided to go to college and helped her make her choice of the best among the Southern colleges for women. She hoped that she could live up to her father's high hopes for her, resolved that she would never disappoint him. (The memory of that resolve was to come to her with sorrow ten years later when she had to send him a message from prison.)

Anne spent the years of the war against Hitler at Randolph-Macon College in the hills of Virginia. It was here that she heard segregation seriously questioned by some of the teachers and one or two of the girls. She read articles in the Richmond paper, editorials by Virginius Dabney, a Southerner, suggesting that "modification of complete separation of the races might be advisable," and pieces in the New York Sunday *Times* that went slightly further. She read a few poems written by Negro poets like Langston Hughes. All her pent-up feelings from childhood shouted "yes!" to *Let America Be America*. It wasn't true that Negro people were happy behind the wall set up by good people like her parents.

In Anne's senior year at Randolph-Macon, a classmate from New York invited her to visit for spring vacation. They had acted together in the Drama Club and she was also one of the girls to whom Anne had talked about what she called the "Negro problem." In New York this friend offered to introduce Anne to an actress in a play on Broadway—a beautiful girl, she said, and a Negro.

The three girls had lunch together in a good restaurant.

"I'm eating with a colored girl!" Anne said to herself, her heart pounding with the excitement of breaking the taboo of a lifetime.

This meeting between two Southerners, one fair, the other dark of skin, was a turning point in Anne's life, but she did not mention this moment of freedom once she was back home again on the white side of the segregation wall.

After college there was every reason for Anne to go back to Anniston and settle down as an attractive, popular member of the younger set at the country club, as a devout and earnest church worker in her spare time—working for brotherhood everywhere but in the colored part of her own town. She did just that for a few months, but she couldn't seem to forget the voice or the brown-skinned sculptured face of the competent young actress. "If she were here—right in Anniston—she'd be in colored town and I could never have met her." In her room at home, in the darkness of night, Anne slowly came to the conclusion that segregation was intolerable.

"As bad," she said to herself, "for my own kind of people as for the Negroes whom we oppress." (Anne didn't say "whom *they* oppress." It was always "we." As a white Southerner she assumed her share of the blame.)

She tried working for a few months on the local newspaper, but she realized that she could stay at home no longer, soothing her conscience with vague thoughts about doing something to help the Negroes. It apparently never occurred to her to escape the problem by running North or to some foreign country as a few young people in Anniston had done. Her flight was only sixty miles away to Birmingham, where she took the same kind of job she had in Anniston, as a reporter on the evening newspaper.

Birmingham was a large, comparatively new industrial city, but in every respect committed to the Southern way of life. Anne could not have chosen a better place to complete her education. As she was alone and knew no one to whom she could talk freely, her work on the paper filled her life. The routine of her day was to leave her boardinghouse room early, to stop at a cafeteria for a cup of coffee before it was time to call the police department to see if any spectacular crime had taken place in the night—anything that ought to be phoned to the copy writer at the paper. When the courts opened she would take her place at the press table to listen to the administration of justice, "Southern style."

In her book, *The Wall Between,* published years later, Anne set down her impression of those courts.

> In covering the Birmingham courthouse, I soon learned that there were two kinds of justice, one for whites and one for Negroes. If a Negro killed a white man, that was a capital crime; if a white man killed a Negro, there were usually "extenuating circumstances" if not outright justification; if a Negro killed a Negro that was just a "nigger" murder—worth at most a year or so in prison. . . . Over the door of the Birmingham courthouse, as on many courthouses, are inscribed the words of Thomas Jefferson: "equal and exact justice to all men of whatever state or persuasion." I read it every morning as I entered the building; I could no longer bear to read the words.

Anne had worked as a police reporter for some months, more and more disturbed that she could think of no way to make the least change in the conditions. She had heard of no group in the city interested in what the Northern papers called "civil rights."

"There must be some people in Birmingham who would care," she said to herself. But if there were, she didn't know how to find them. And of course she was not acquainted with any Negroes at all.

One morning she stopped as usual for coffee and sat at a table with another reporter. They talked shop and he told a few amusing anecdotes. Suddenly she looked at her watch. It was time to check with the police sergeant. She left the table, went to make her call in the phone booth. When she returned, a Negro waitress was refilling the coffee cups.

"Anything doing?" her companion asked.

"No. Everything quiet. Nothing but a colored murder on Eighteenth Street."

*Nothing but!* Even as the words fell from her lips, she became aware of how they must sound to the young waitress, pouring coffee into her cup. Anne was the white world speaking, the world to whom the death of a Negro meant nothing. She had voiced the thinking of Birmingham, that the killing of a Negro by another Negro was not news. . . . "Segregation isn't a wall; it's an octopus," she said to herself, feeling strangled as she forced herself to look at the waitress. Dare she try to explain?

The girl's face was without expression, her eyes on the cup. But her hand holding the coffeepot was rigid. The cup overflowed and a few brown drops spilled on the table.

Anne didn't try to say anything. Words were useless. "No white person in the South can remain neutral," she said to herself. As long as she did not *act* to change the system, words like justice and freedom simply poisoned the air.

But Anne couldn't think of anything practical to do— alone. Again she fled—not out of the South—never away from the South. The problem was *here*. She took a job as copy writer on the Louisville, Kentucky, *Times*.

Louisville was by all tradition a Southern city, but the newspaper was owned by two men who were well known for their position against segregation of the races. Partly through the efforts of Barry Bingham and Mark Ethridge, Louisville had a reputation of being a place where progress was being made.

When she first got there, it seemed a world of miracles to Anne. She had been born in Kentucky, but her parents had moved away when she was an infant. First Mississippi and then Alabama had been her environment. Compared to these places, the city of Louisville was indeed a miracle. When she rode to work on a bus in the morning, Negroes got on and sat wherever they wanted to. The university and the libraries were open to everyone. And Negroes voted without hindrance—enough of them so that they had come to have some power in the city. When their leaders spoke on a subject of interest, what they had to say was newsworthy and came to her desk to be written up: *Mr. so-and-so of the NAACP expressed himself as favoring such-and-such a piece of legislation.* In Louisville you could call colored people Mr. or Mrs. and by their last names!

The NAACP had a mixed membership, mostly Negroes but a sprinkling of white people. Anne joined at once and went to her first meeting with another member of the newspaper staff by the name of Carl Braden. She was already falling in love with Carl. He was ten years older than she was and he lived on the wrong side of the tracks and didn't belong to the country club or to the Episcopal Church. He didn't belong to any church; his mother was a Catholic and his father, when he was alive, had been an agnostic and a Debs socialist. "But there wasn't any friction in the family," Carl said with the twinkle in his eyes she found irresistible. "Both the church and Debs taught brotherhood. That was good enough for me."

Carl was against anything that prevented equality for all people, but he had not the intense interest in breaking down the wall of segregation that had become Anne's primary object in life. Carl, who had known what it was to go hungry as a boy, was deeply dedicated to raising the living standards of working people, black or white. To him the answer to almost everything was strong trade unions.

After they were married, Carl and Anne shared each other's concerns. In the CIO unions Anne found not only Negroes but white people who were willing to take a stand against segregation. And seeing the life of the Negro people through Anne's eyes, Carl became aware that Louisville, forward-looking at it was, had a long way to go before Negroes of the city could live on a basis of true equality.

The Bradens joined every organization, every committee within and outside the trade-union movement that gave promise of improved conditions. They worked successfully to open the private hospitals to Negro patients and to allow Negro women to take nurses' training. They worked to let everyone use *all* of the parks and recreational facilities; they worked on an interracial committee to desegregate the public schools. In each of these campaigns they had the support of the newspaper. The Louisville *Times* and the morning paper, the *Enquirer,* published under the same liberal ownership, believed in a quiet one-job-at-a-time approach to integration. It seemed a slow method to Anne and to some of the Negro people who had waited so long for the freedom to go where they wanted to, live where they wanted—the freedom which the whites accepted as a matter of course.

The desegregation of Louisville did not go very deep. It stopped short, for instance, at the point of letting Negroes buy a house anywhere that suited them. Almost ten years had gone by since the war and still no new housing had been constructed except in neighborhoods where custom and the Real Estate Board made it impossible for a colored family to buy. The black population was crammed into a slum section near the center of town or into a few scattered blocks backed up against the banks of the Ohio River.

This was near the area where Carl and Anne had bought a small cottage. It had once been the best residential district, but as people built new homes for themselves or bought houses put up by builders out in the suburbs, the old houses in several blocks in the area had been sold to Negroes. "Block-busting," the real estate people called it. First they'd move one Negro family in and then go from house to house, playing on old prejudices, on a fear of falling values, getting families to put their homes up for sale and move away. Then the deserted houses would be sold to other Negro families at higher prices.

Anne had watched the block in back of theirs being "busted." She was digusted at the methods used, but pleased to be living in a mixed neighborhood. The Braden children, Jimmy, aged two, and year-old Anita, would have colored children as well as whites among their playmates.

Anne and Carl had left the paper for a year to work in the public relations department of one of the CIO unions. They had both enjoyed the work, but when Jimmy was born Anne stayed home and Carl went back to the paper, this time as copy writer for the *Enquirer*. Anne kept up her activities with the NAACP, the Urban League and other groups. Their home was a meeting place for Negroes and whites alike; but she loved having time to play with Jimmy, to care for the baby, to cook Carl's favorite dishes for the evenings he was home for supper and, above all, time to make friends in the mixed neighborhood.

So on the afternoon when an NAACP acquaintance of

theirs, Andrew Wade, came by to ask if she and Carl would be willing to buy a house out in one of the new suburbs and sell it back to him to live in, Anne suggested that she could find a house near theirs.

But Andrew said no, that wasn't what his wife wanted.

"Charlotte has her heart set on a new, stone ranch house in one of the developments in the country. We've got a little girl just about the age of Jimmy and another one on the way. We've been looking for a home for over two years," he added. "The ones Charlotte likes are always in the wrong neighborhood. You know how it is, real estate men won't show those houses to colored people. The banks won't approve the loans. It's tough. A colored real estate man, a friend of mine, said the thing to do was to get some white family to buy the house, me putting up the down payment of course, and then deed it to us."

"You might run into unfriendly neighbors," Carl said. "Had you considered that?"

"We've considered everything," the young veteran answered gravely. "We can take a few rebuffs. They'll come around when the strangeness wears off. There's no other way. I tried a couple of other white friends, people I've known longer than I have you folks. For one reason or another, they didn't see their way clear to make the purchase for me. I don't want you to, if you'd rather not. But it would sure be a favor."

Anne and Carl exchanged glances. Anne nodded.

"Of course we'll do it," Carl said.

When Andrew had gone, Anne commented that a ranch house with a picture window was not the kind of house she'd choose for herself, but if Mrs. Wade wanted it that's what she ought to have. "What we're doing is legal, isn't it?" she remembered to ask. "It's a technique that's been used in several places."

"Certainly," Carl answered, and went back to the book he was reading to Jimmy.

Two months went by before the Wades had settled on the house they wanted and brought the $1400 for the down payment.

"The place is exactly what Charlotte wants—ranch style, picture window and all—and plenty of room for our little girl to run and play. It's in Shively—not one of the fancy suburbs, but quiet and real pretty. The road in front of the house isn't paved yet—only two houses are finished besides ours—Charlotte's and mine."

On May 10, 1954, all the preliminary arrangements had been made for the purchase. Anne and Carl went with a white real estate man to the bank to close the deal. There they met Mr. James I. Rone, the owner and builder. He was not a professional contractor, he explained, just built houses on Rone Court near his own home and sold them as they were built—did the work in his spare time. He was very friendly. Anne realized that he was greeting them, not only as buyers of the house he had for sale on a dead-end street he had proudly named for himself, but as future neighbors.

It was a bad moment. She had never deceived anybody before in her life. Then she set her mind firmly on Andrew Wade, and on an endless procession of Negroes over history who had been denied their rights. The least she could do— as a white Southerner—was to help get this one man a house to live in. In silence she watched Carl turn over Andrew's money. She signed her name where she was told to. The keys were handed over and Rone left to take the deed to the court-house to be recorded. This was their crime, for which their lives would be threatened, for which they would be made the objects of hatred and scorn, for which they would spend time in prison.

When Carl and Anne left the bank, events moved swiftly. They drove to the Wades' with the keys of his house and then to Rone Court with Andrew Wade. Mrs. Rone was there, scrubbing the "For Sale" sign off the window. She didn't question Andrew's presence—probably thought he had come to get the house ready for the Bradens to move into.

Andrew was at the house every day, waxing floors and re-painting a room or two to suit his wife's color scheme. No one bothered him. It is possible (for he was quite fair skinned) that no one realized at first that he was a Negro. But on Thursday, Rone approached Andrew and asked rather belliger-ently whether the Bradens were renting the house to him.

"No," Andrew answered. "They are deeding it to me."

"Deeding it to you? Who is?" Rone's eyes were bulging.

"Why, Mr. and Mrs. Braden. They're the ones who own it, aren't they?"

Rone dashed out of the house, speechless, and Andrew went back to his painting. At suppertime he went home to get his wife. They were going to do some work on the floors together that night. When the Wades returned, the Rone yard was full of cars, and men and women were milling around.

"Don't worry, Charlotte. They're surprised and have to get used to the idea of having us in the neighborhood. We'll stay right here." Andrew had been in tighter spots in the war.

Nothing happened at the Wades', and about eleven the cars began driving away. "You see?" Wade said as he started his own car to drive Charlotte home.

But the mob had decided to attack the man they considered responsible for the outrage—Carl Braden. The knock came on his door around midnight. The driveway and the street were blocked with cars. James Rone and Hudson, the real estate agent, were on the front porch, backed up by a threatening crowd of men and women.

In answer to their question Carl said, yes, he had sold the

house to Mr. Wade. Yes, Wade and his wife were colored. There were angry cries of "Get those people out of Rone Court!"

A red-faced blonde pushed forward and threatened Carl's own house, his children. Carl stiffened and ordered the crowd off his property. He'd be glad, he said to Rone, to talk the matter over calmly any time he chose to come back and act like a gentleman. After more threats about what they'd do if the Wades weren't out of the house by tomorrow, the crowd drifted away.

Carl had been alone in the house, except for the sleeping children. Anne came home from a meeting and the Wades drove up shortly afterward.

Anne felt sorry for James Rone when she heard about the midnight visit. His neighbors were probably blaming him. She had known people like him all her life. The mere presence of people like Andrew and Charlotte had brought his world down about his ears. But her heart went out to Charlotte even more. Andrew could take trouble; Charlotte was not a fighter. She had lived behind the wall of segregation all her life and hadn't known what it might take to break through.

The next day Rone and his son came to Wade and tried to buy the house back. Andrew refused and tried to explain that all he wanted was a good house to live in, that they didn't have to be friends. "I'm an American citizen, like you are. I fought for my country. I'm a person like you. Does it mean I can't live where I want to because my skin is a different color from yours? We can all get along in the same world. To me, that's what democracy means."

The son seemed at the time to understand. But that night he was with the mob that gathered and burned a big cross in the yard. Rifle shots came through the window and lodged in the woodwork.

Anne and Carl had been kept awake half the night by telephone calls: *Get those blacks out. Get the Wades off of Rone Court.*

The news of the cross burning and shots would be in the papers next day. In the morning, while the incessant calls continued, Carl wrote out a statement telling why he and Anne had thought it right to do what they did: "We feel that every man has a right to live where he wants, regardless of the color of his skin. This is the test of democracy. Either you practice what you preach or you shut up about believing in democracy."

Anne phoned every minister and priest in the neighborhood of the Wade house, explained the situation and asked them to help calm the neighbors' baseless fears. Every one of the churchmen expressed sympathy, but each man had a different reason for refusing.

"I don't mind going," one said. "But if I go, people in my church will turn against me." Burning the cross was an un-Christian act, said another, but he had no church members in the area. A third was afraid of destroying his influence for other worth-while causes. A fourth was from the North and people would not like his interfering in a Southern problem.

It wasn't that the Wades lacked support. They had it from their own people—from the NAACP, the Negro churches, the editor of the Negro paper. The leaders of the black community formed a Wade Defense Committee and made the Wades' cause their own. But Anne knew that this was not a battle that the Negroes could win by themselves. They were too few. It would take white support to turn the tide of public opinion. Labor leaders Carl approached promised to bring the case up at the next union meetings; but it was a hard issue for labor to fight—if it were jobs, it would be different. And the white liberals on whom Anne thought she could count, with whom she had worked on other campaigns, said housing was different. Friends in her church were against segregation,

of course; but buying a house for the sole purpose of trans-
ferring it to a Negro family was a blunder. It was too sudden
a move. One must go forward gradually, as Louisville had
always done.

The Wades stuck it out. Friends, mostly Negro from the
Defense Committee aided by a few whites, guarded the house
night and day. Inside, Charlotte Wade went on quietly making
curtains and putting paper on the shelves and arranging her
pretty china.

Anne took the children out sometimes to visit her, but
mostly she spent her time phoning and writing letters—and
receiving threats to herself and Carl and her children on the
telephone. A Miss Gilbert and her friend, Miss La Rue, were
a great help to her. Miss Gilbert was a social worker and a
member of the Women's International League for Peace and
Freedom, and she wrote a letter to the papers in the name of
the league. When the bank called the loan on the mortgage,
Miss Gilbert helped Anne try to find a new mortgagee, though
in the end it was a Negro who came forward with the
necessary loan.

At the end of June, on the first evening the Wades had
relaxed enough to go out to a little picnic in a park by the
river, a bomb was exploded under the house. It shattered the
bedroom wing. If the Wades had been at home they would
probably have been killed. The guard that night was outside
on the porch and escaped injury.

Charlotte moved back to town to her mother's, but Andrew
would not budge. "I'll live here or I'll die here," he said. He
stayed every night until midnight all summer long. Sometimes
the Bradens rode out to keep him company.

Meanwhile the county police were supposedly looking for
the bombers. Once it was rumored they had a confession and
only needed a little more evidence to go before the Grand
Jury. The Defense Committee kept urging action. The

violently reactionary weekly paper in the Shively suburb kept up a counter-campaign that was beginning to have its desired effect. It was the editor's theory that the purchase of the house for the Wades was simply part of a country-wide Communist plot to overthrow the government. It was, the editor declared, a well-known fact that Roosevelt and Truman and President Eisenhower were all Communists. The Bradens and all the whites who had come to the aid of the Negro couple must be too. Andrew Wade and his wife were just victims. Communists had made him buy the house and blown it up themselves to make trouble and overthrow the Government of the Sovereign State of Kentucky.

Anne had heard talk like this before, during the war, when the Anniston ladies were so furious about the "Eleanor Clubs" their servants were supposed to have formed; but it worried her and saddened her, too. She was relieved when the prosecuting attorney announced in the fall that he was ready to go before the Grand Jury with the case of the Wade bombing. She and Carl were among the witnesses called to testify. So were Miss La Rue and Miss Gilbert, as well as a truck driver by the name of Bown, who had helped guard the Wades' home from time to time.

There were two ideas about the bombing, the prosecuting attorney explained as he opened the hearing. One was that neighbors of the Negro family had done it to drive the Wades out of the neighborhood. The other was that it was perhaps an inside job, carried out by friends of the Wades—maybe even a Communist plot to create an incident and make trouble. In fact, he said in the calm, courteous voice of the Southern gentleman that he was, perhaps the whole idea of the Wades moving to Rone Court had been dreamed up by Mr. and Mrs. Braden, who planned it and told the innocent colored people what to do. As time went on, A. Scott Hamilton, the prosecuting attorney, concluded, he was inclined more and more to the second theory. But of course the gentlemen of the jury were the ones to decide.

He turned suavely to Anne. "Mrs. Braden, will you take the witness stand."

The rest of the hearing before the Grand Jury was a long nightmare. Hamilton had dredged up an ancient "sedition law" which never in all its history had been put to use. Under this law he requested indictments of Anne and Carl. Miss La Rue and Miss Gilbert were indicted for contempt of court for refusing to answer questions. Bown was charged with the actual bombing, although the astonished truck driver could prove he had been driving a load in his truck into the Middle West the night the house was destroyed.

Carl was imprisoned at once to await trial. The bail set was so large that there was no hope of raising the amount. When Anne knew the warrant would be issued for her arrest, she mailed a letter to her parents explaining what had happened. She wrote that she knew that they disapproved of her work against segregation, so she did not want to involve them in her trouble. At the end of the letter she added: "Don't come up here. Don't call. Write me if you want to. If you don't, I will understand."

They did come to take the children home to Anniston. Quietly Anne closed the house and called a taxi to go to the police station. Her bail was set at $10,000. She had little hope of raising it, but after she had spent seven days in the jail, her lawyer came to her with the news that a friend of her father's had offered to make bond. She accepted with the proviso that it was understood that she would not change her views on segregation.

The five under indictment had no lack of lawyers to act in their defense. At long last the *Enquirer* and the liberals were aroused. Carl's trial opened in November. He was convicted and sentenced to prison for fifteen years, and was sent back to prison to await appeal. Trial of the others was postponed, pending the outcome of Carl's appeal. This time his bail was set at $40,000.

Anne was numb by this time, almost beyond suffering. She had seen Negroes sentenced unjustly so many times—in Anniston, in Birmingham. Now it was her turn and Carl's. . . . They *were* guilty, not of the crime as charged, but of trying to break down a wall so high, so long in building.

Carl Braden remained in prison—part of the time in solitary confinement—for a year until his bail was collected almost dollar by dollar from people all over the nation. In April 1956 the case Scott Hamilton had so skillfully built out of myth was reversed. Now Carl was *really* free. And Anne was never tried. The children were home, the family in their home together once more.

Anne set down their experience in a book, *The Wall Between,* which has been called a classic by critics. Neither Anne nor Carl gave up the struggle. Neither left the South. The Southwide interracial organization, the Southern Conference Educational Fund, which had begun its work in 1938 as a wing of the Southern Conference for Human Welfare was quietly building support among whites and Negroes for the new day whose dawn was the 1954 Supreme Court decision against segregated schools. The director, Jim Dombrowski, had need for people like the Bradens. Carl became a fieldworker for the organization, and Anne became staff writer on the monthly paper, the *Southern Patriot.*

The headquarters of the Southern Educational Conference was New Orleans, but the Bradens were able to carry on their work from Louisville. They were close to the leaders of the Negro liberation movement, close to the students of both races on the picket lines.

When Jim Dombrowski retired from the directorship in 1964, Carl Braden took his place as director. Anne became the editor of the *Southern Patriot*. The headquarters was moved to Louisville. The new president of the organization is, interestingly, from Birmingham—the intrepid Negro minister Fred Shuttlesworth, who with Dr. Martin Luther King, Jr., led the historic Easter march in his city in 1963.

And the Wade house? Andrew Wade had begun slowly to rebuild the shattered wing. In another year it was in beautiful repair. But it could never be a home, his wife said—not after everything that had happened. In the spring of 1957, Andrew came to tell the Bradens that he had put a "For Sale" sign in the front yard.

# 10 Uphill all the way

"We come now to the hour in our history when we must choose between segregation and democracy. Shall we adopt segregation of the races as the bedrock and cling to it at all costs? Shall we abandon democratic processes in our national government just so we retain segregation?" In these words Judge Lee Ward of Arkansas summed up the significance of the decision of the Supreme Court of the United States declaring unconstitutional the segregation of students in public school on the basis of color.

To black Southerners the decision of May 17, 1954, was a day of jubilee to be celebrated as a second Emancipation Proclamation. The Supreme Court had said: "In the field of education 'separate though equal' has no place." Negroes began to hope that the whole struggle for equal citizenship could be won. Segregation in public schools which are supported by compulsory education laws and by taxes paid by everyone was especially humiliating to every parent. It meant that even before they could read, children were excluded from contact with others in the community. To those who knew the history of public education in the Southern states, school segregation brought up unhappy memories. No public schools were in existence in the South until they were established for "black and white alike" by Negro legislators just after the Civil War. When the Reconstruction governments were overturned, the system of free public schools was retained—for

whites alone. Years later schools were opened for Negro children. They were expected to be grateful for the makeshift
schooling in shabby buildings with poor equipment and dis-
carded textbooks. About 1935 the legal department of the
NAACP went to the courts to seek a remedy for the inade-
quacies. A few graduate schools were opened to Negro students. Better buildings were built in Southern cities and
Negro teachers were given equal pay with white teachers.
Then had come the 1954 decision banning separate schools.
The order was to be carried out "with all deliberate speed."

However, the walls of segregation did not come tumbling
down. One year, two years went by and less than 2 per cent
of the segregated white schools had allowed a child with dark
skin to enter their doors. In the Deep South parents took the
risk of losing jobs or of personal injury to bring law suits to
force compliance of the 1954 Supreme Court decision. It was
an uphill fight. The NAACP and other national interracial
organizations tried to get Southern whites to help them
build a better climate of opinion. Their efforts only roused
echoes of "Yankee meddling" of the 1860s and 1870s. A
sprinkling of Southern-born white moderates—ministers, a
few writers such as Lillian Smith and John Howard Griffin,
newspapermen like Harry Ashmore and Ralph McGill wrote
or spoke with their friends or preached from pulpits. It didn't
matter that they were Southern-born. Like every other white
person in Southern history the voices of these moderates who
suggested that there might be justice in the court's decision
were not heard above the tumult raised by the members of
the revived Ku Klux Klan or the White Citizens' Council.
By the summer of 1957, when courts urged that there be no
more delay, a troubled citizenship saw the enrollment of
even five or six dark-skinned pupils in a "white" school as an
intolerable invasion.

A sense of frustration added to the mob spirit. After all
the violent effort spent in keeping the Negro in his place,

children, with the backing of the Federal government dared . . .

For it was the children and only the children upon whom the responsibility fell. Anxious parents were relegated to the background. The Negro and white leaders who, for the sake of America's future, for the ideals of the Declaration of Independence, for the sake of freedom had urged this attack on racial discrimination, could only watch the struggle from the sidelines. The adults had to step back and leave it to children to take the final step across the threshold of a hostile school—or in a Little Rock high school in the fall of 1957 to be turned away by white militia "with bayonets at the ready."

# Dunbar
# Ogden

The Ogdens were still at supper when the telephone rang.

"I'll get it, Dad," David said.

Mrs. Ogden relaxed as David made his way through the old-fashioned arch into the living room. Her twenty-one-year-old son was a comfort to have at home. He understood so well that his father must be protected from the impossible demands a congregation made on a minister. She smiled across the oval table at her handsome, graying husband.

There was no answering smile in Dunbar Ogden's eyes. He was intent on the muted voice of the news commentator on the radio.

> Governor Faubus says the inevitable conclusion is that our Little Rock schools must be operated as they have in the past. Central High will open tomorrow morning protected from trouble by our own National Guard. I repeat, Central High will open for the regularly enrolled white students tomorrow morning.

"For you, Dad." There was a note of excitement in David's voice. "I think you'd better take it. It's a—a Mrs. Bates."

"Bates?" There was no such name on his parish rolls. Dunbar Ogden pushed his chair back resignedly. Mrs. Ogden snapped off the radio and began shamelessly to eavesdrop.

"Yes? . . . Mrs. L. C. Bates? Oh, Daisy Bates? Of the NAACP?" A long pause. And then Dunbar Ogden spoke again. "You want me to walk? . . . I see. Of course, I am sympathetic. But . . . Yes, I'll give it careful consideration . . . I appreciate your calling."

There was a strange expression on the Reverend Ogden's face as he came back to the table. Silently he sat down and began to sip his fresh-poured coffee. His wife and older son waited none too patiently.

"That was Daisy Bates—Mrs. Bates she calls herself—of the Arkansas State NAACP. She was calling to tell me that the Negroes have decided to send their children to Central High in spite of Faubus' recommendation and—"

David gave a low whistle. Mrs. Ogden opened her mouth to say something but changed her mind.

"—they want me, as president of the Ministerial Alliance, to escort the children to school tomorrow."

"Good deal!" David was enthusiastic. "Listen, I'm going with you! After all, I'm bigger than you, and if anything happens . . ."

Mrs. Ogden lifted the silver coffeepot to refill her cup. Her hand trembled. Why Dunbar? Why place her husband in this difficult position? If the Negroes were going through with this and needed outside support why hadn't they gone to Mr. Ashmore? Harry Ashmore had printed editorials in the *Gazette* urging Little Rock to integrate its schools, or Mrs. Bates could have called that radical teacher at the Negro college.

"David, wait." Mr. Ogden broke in sharply. "I don't know whether I'm going to accompany those children or not, son. You see, there are so many things . . . I just don't know."

As president of the Ministerial Alliance of Little Rock, Arkansas, Dunbar Ogden should have been able to answer yes or no to Mrs. Bates' request. The trouble hadn't come to Little Rock suddenly. The members of his congregation who knew and loved him as a true Southern gentleman certainly had a right to expect from him a polite but firm refusal. So would anyone who knew the background and traditions of this fifty-five-year-old representative of the Ogden family of Mississippi.

Dunbar Henry Ogden had been born in 1903 in Columbus, Mississippi, where his father was pastor of the Presbyterian Church. Columbus had little of the wealth or glamor of Natchez, where the Ogden mansion stood, still as stately as it had been generations before when slaves had tended the house and grounds. The Manse, as the home provided for the young minister was called, was small and a little run-down. But Dunbar's mother made it lovely with the Dunbar rosewood furniture and ornaments and all the gracious manners of the "Southern way of life."

The public school in Columbus (though for whites only,

of course) was not considered an appropriate place for a descendant of the Ogdens and the Dunbars to begin his education. For the years that he lived in Columbus, Dunbar's mother taught him at home.

After the spelling and geography and number work were over, she talked to him often about his glorious heritage and about his responsibility to help the poor and the suffering. She read stories from the Bible or from leatherbound books of poetry. He came to know the Southern poets Paul Hamilton Hayne and Sidney Lanier. Tennyson's poems about Sir Galahad and the rest of the Knights of the Round Table, with their high ideals and noble language, became part of his heritage, too.

There were more recent books as well—the plantation stories of Thomas Nelson Page and Joel Chandler Harris. "Billy" and "Uncle Remus," the faithful slaves of bygone days, were more real to the little boy than the Negroes who moved like shadows along the streets of Columbus. With them he had no contact whatsoever. Except as servants, they were never seen in his home, in the parks where he played or in his father's church.

After a few years in Columbus, Dunbar's father was called to preach in other churches—in Knoxville, Tennessee, then Atlanta, Georgia. In Atlanta, the boy went to a public high school, then away to Davidson College and the Richmond theological seminary to become a minister like his father. Later he held pastorates in various towns and cities, all in the South except one. In every Southern city where he was known, the Reverend Dunbar Ogden, Jr., was well liked for his kindness and charm, and looked up to for his aristocratic Southern family background.

Ogden had been called to the Central Presbyterian Church in Little Rock in January 1954. He had preached there only a few months when the Supreme Court ruling against segregated schools was announced. The members of his congregation were happy in this moment of crisis that their new minister was from Mississippi, a Southerner from the Deep South. They liked his courtly manners, his soft-voiced eloquence. They felt sure he would sympathize with their unwillingness to turn their backs on all they had been taught to believe. Besides, he had children of his own, a grown son in the Army, a second son, David, almost through college and then the twins. Mr. Ogden could be depended on. He would be the last person, they told themselves, to want his children to go to school with "those people."

Background, custom, tradition and the community in which he had his church all prompted Dunbar Ogden, Jr., to say no to the Negro woman on the telephone on the evening of September 3, 1957. Why then had he hesitated?

The summer that Dunbar Ogden was eight was spent in Natchez in the home of his grandparents. Here, for the first time, he had a "best friend." Jim lived on the edge of town on his family's plantation, and Dunbar was invited to spend a week at his home. A wonderful week of fishing and trapping rabbits and roaming the place—the two eight-year-olds in the company of a slightly older Negro boy they called Snowball.

Playing with the Negro lad was a new experience for Dunbar. The only colored people who had entered his life until now were a succession of cooks in Mother's kitchen, the old man his father spoke of as the yard "boy," and the washwoman's husband who brought the basket of clean clothes to the back door every Friday.

Snowball was different. The three boys had played together all week on equal—or almost equal—terms. Of course when they went fishing it was Snowball who carried the lard can of worms for bait. He baited their hooks, and if they were lucky enough to catch any fish, Snowball cleaned them and started the fire to cook them right there on the creek bank.

Snowball knew how to set rabbit traps. It was only when they were seeing who was *best* that the colored boy never came out ahead. Like racing or wrestling, when Jim could always get him down and make him cry uncle.

The week was almost at an end. Jim and Dunbar were lying under the shade of a tree catching their breath after a race across the lawn. Dunbar watched Snowball loping toward the kitchen door.

"Jim, I've been wondering . . . How come Snowball always comes in last?"

"What do you mean, last?" Jim mumbled. He had discovered a piece of sour grass and was sucking the juice out of the stem.

"Well, Snowball's bigger'n we are. His legs are a heap longer," Dunbar persisted. "By rights he ought'a beat us— racin' or wrestlin' or jumpin' or anything. But he never has, not one time."

Jim turned over lazily. "You're crazier'n a grasshopper. Snowball can outrun or outjump any boy this side of Natchez. He can lick 'em, too. But Snowball's my *boy*. Naturally he can't beat me nor you neither, Dunbar Ogden."

*Because I'm a Dunbar and an Ogden. Because Great-grandpapa owned the most slaves of anybody in Mississippi. Maybe in the whole South. Because we're white and any white person is better than any black, whatever they do.*

Jim's explanation was perfectly sensible. It fit in with everything the little Ogden boy had ever heard.

And yet—*was it fair?*

A little red in the face, Dunbar let the thought die unspoken. And just to be sure that questions of "right" and "fair" didn't rise up to pester him again he began to tease Snowball when the boy came back from the kitchen with a pitcher of lemonade and a gourd dipper.

"Snowball! That's sure a funny name!"

After a pause the boy said uneasily, "Enoch's the name my pappy give me."

"Enoch?" Dunbar sat up straight in surprise. "That's a *Bible* name." It had never occurred to him that *colored* people might know the Bible and pray to the same God his father preached about. Was it possible that in spite of their black skin Negroes were the children of God?

Dunbar's father was transferred that winter to Knoxville, and though the boy spent several more vacations in Natchez, he never saw the Negro lad again.

"Where's Enoch?" he asked the next time he visited at Jim's plantation.

"You mean old Snowball? He's not around any more. Papa had to put his family off the place. They got kinda uppity—always talking about wanting to go somewhere North. Birmingham or Chicago, I don't know. Mississippi wasn't good enough for 'em."

Dunbar's questions were soon forgotten. His moment of doubt lay buried deep, and the way of the white South was still the right way, the only way.

When he went to the public high school in Atlanta, he was younger both in years and experience than most of the class and never managed to become one of the gang.

"The boys in public school haven't had your advantages," his father pointed out. "It will be different when you get to college and join the fraternity."

The fraternity! Mr. Ogden didn't say "a" fraternity. There was only one he had in mind—his own, to which all the Dunbar and Ogden cousins belonged.

Davidson College and the fraternity were worth waiting for.

"And after Davidson, I'll go to Union Theological at Richmond," the boy said cheerfully. He had never given a thought to being anything but a minister.

Already he taught Sunday school in his father's church, and in his senior year at high school somebody suggested that he go across town and hold a class for colored children.

"It is true," his mother said, "that the colored people are destined to be hewers of wood and drawers of water. But they must be treated with kindliness, and to teach a Sunday school over there would be a kindly deed."

World War I had just ended and the streets of Atlanta were full of returning soldiers. Dunbar envied the young officers receiving smart salutes, the enlisted men in their jaunty khaki.

Of course, some of the khaki-clad boys were just "red necks" from the cotton mills. And some, he realized as he got into the colored section, were Negroes. To see colored boys in the uniform made him vaguely uneasy. They strutted along the middle of the sidewalk as if they no longer knew their place.

After teaching the class, Dunbar decided to take a bus home. While he was waiting on the corner a phrase from the Sunday school lesson kept running through his mind: *The stone that the builder rejected shall become the chief cornerstone.* He had explained carefully how God had his own ways of choosing different from man's. "Do you understand?" he had asked. They had nodded their heads obediently. But the whole lesson was probably beyond their understanding.

As the bus rolled up, a small incident occurred. Four or five people got on. A colored soldier with a lot of stripes on his sleeves was in the line. The conductor called to him to step aside.

"Can't you see there's white folks waiting, you black so-and-so?"

Dunbar saw the soldier's black eyes snap in anger, his right hand double into a threatening black fist. It looked as if there might be trouble. But the door clanged shut and the bus started slowly to roll.

"Put 'em in uniform and there's no holding 'em," the conductor muttered.

Dunbar, staring through the window, saw the soldier's fist open limply, the shoulders sag under the khaki shirt. He felt a moment of compassion . . . *the stone that the builder rejected* . . . But the conductor was right, of course. You couldn't have colored people crowding ahead of whites.

Before he reached home, the incident was forgotten.

A year later, Dunbar was at Davidson College, two hundred miles from Atlanta. It was spring and it was pledge day for the fraternities. You could feel the tingling excitement all over the campus, and Dunbar's heart was pounding as he started for his first class. Before night he'd be a fraternity man like his father and cousins before him. How long he had waited for this day!

Then at dusk, standing with clenched fists by his window, he faced the truth. Pledge day had come and gone with no invitation from his father's fraternity or any other. He, Dunbar Ogden, had been passed over, rejected. His hand opened limply and he leaned against the window.

Suddenly every line of that black soldier's sagging body came before his eyes. For one moment he knew exactly how it felt when an iron door clanged shut in your face. With no conscious memory of the Atlanta incident, he identified himself for an instant with the unknown Negro—then fiercely his Southern-bred mind rejected the fleeting identity with the "inferior race."

To cover his sense of rejection, he set about with a kind of bravado to become a leader among the non-fraternity students. He thought up all kinds of pranks and even staged a mock lynching on campus with an obliging janitor as the victim. It was all in good fun, and if the Negro had any thoughts except being pleased to earn a dollar just for posing with a rope around his neck, Dunbar and his friends didn't hear them expressed.

Three years later, the disappointment of his freshman year at Davidson had worn off. At theological school there were no fraternities. There was no question of Dunbar's acceptance among the serious young men preparing for the ministry. He sang in the choir and heard for the first time really fine music.

One day after choir practice the director suggested that they go down to a Negro church to hear some old slavery spirituals.

"You'll find them quaint and primitive, but rather interesting," the director explained.

Dunbar was more than interested; he was deeply stirred. There was nothing quaint about those harmonies, and for all the bad grammar the words were *poetry*.

Dunbar was groping for understanding of the part of the human race that was somehow pitiful because inferior. He heard of a college for Negroes across town in Richmond and felt a curiosity to see what educated Negroes were like. He visited the campus and got into conversation with one or two students. But he came away feeling that colored people were hard to talk to, that somehow they didn't appreciate his well-meant interest.

Dunbar Ogden's first church was in the North Carolina mountains. After that he preached in a couple of Southern cities before being called to a small town in Ohio.

"Our Ministerial Alliance is interracial," the Ohio head of the Alliance explained uneasily when he invited the young Southerner to join.

"Colored and white meeting together?" After a moment's struggle Southern manners won out over Southern customs and the Reverend Ogden graciously accepted the invitation.

Dunbar felt thoroughly uncomfortable at first, sitting

around a table with Negroes. After a few months he got used to it, though he was careful not to mention, on his visits South, that black and white drank tea together at the close of the monthly gatherings.

Dunbar married an Ohio girl and shortly afterward was called to preside over one of the largest churches in Staunton, Virginia. The country was in the grip of the Great Depression, when one out of every five families in the South had no breadwinner and hunger was stalking the land. In Staunton, Dunbar did a daring thing. He helped organize an interracial conference of ministers to discuss unemployment relief. Through this and through his love of singing, he became acquainted with a Negro minister whom he liked to think of as his friend.

Reverend Lee called at the Ogden house several times on matters of relief, and gradually the tall, brown-skinned man took to staying for an hour or so after the business was concluded. Mrs. Ogden played the piano and the three of them sang. Sometimes they just talked—about books, about baseball, about things President Roosevelt was doing in Washington.

After a year or so, Lee moved away and they never heard from him again. Still, the idea that he had had a Negro for a personal friend was important to Dunbar. He felt that it broadened his outlook, and he had genuinely enjoyed knowing Reverend Lee. He spoke of "my friend Reverend Lee" as evidence that there were some very fine individuals among the Negroes. It did not occur to him that the friendship was hopelessly limited by his own belief that he belonged to a superior race. Nor did it occur to him that they had never invited Mrs. Lee to visit; in fact, had never met her at all.

The Ogdens, like all decent people, were shocked by the Nazi murder of six million Jews in Europe merely because they *were* Jews. It became the custom in many localities to observe an annual Brotherhood Week dedicated to intergroup understanding. Near the close of World War II, Dunbar was asked to preach the Brotherhood Week sermon at one of the Negro churches. He prepared his sermon with particular care and read it to his wife on Saturday night after the little boys were in bed.

The relations between Negroes and whites in Staunton were a little strained at the time. The Negro people were asking to use the new "white" park, because they had none of their own. There had been quite a stir about the problem. Dunbar had taken as his text: *Render unto Caesar the things that are Caesar's, unto God the things that are God's.* He had developed quite eloquently the beauty of spiritual values, the fellowship of the spirit.

"I wanted them to understand that they'll have to be patient and rise above petty resentment until funds can be raised for a playground in the colored section," he explained.

Sunday morning he stood up to speak in the crowded church. Suddenly before the startled congregation he tore the pages of his sermon in two and as a white man begged forgiveness for the sins of his race.

"I think you should have schools just as good as we have. I think you should have parks just as good, churches as good and good houses and the opportunity to vote." Tears were in his eyes, and he spoke with real sympathy for these victims of injustice who sat before him. But he did not say that they should use the same parks, the same schools, the same churches as the whites. That thought did not come to his mind. But as a compassionate and sensitive person, he was saddened by the thought that he, being white, found himself placed on the side of injustice.

Dunbar Ogden came to Little Rock in 1954 still hoping in his heart that someday—in some far tomorrow—a miracle would occur and that the South he loved so greatly, the white South, would find a way to hold out its hand to the Negro people in brotherhood. Many good things had come about since he was a boy in Mississippi. Surely full justice would come . . . someday.

The Ogdens had barely time to get settled in Little Rock when the Supreme Court of the United States declared that "in the field of education, the doctrine of separate but equal has no place." The Federal courts in the Southern states were charged with the responsibility of carrying out desegregation.

The die-hards shouted "Never!" A handful of foolhardy souls dared to say that the ruling should be put into effect at once. The vast majority whispered, "Not now, not in our time." Tension mounted.

Dunbar's own mind was in a turmoil. There was no one he could talk to—no one. Jonathan, his oldest son, was away in officer's training camp. David, like so many of the young people in high schools and colleges, couldn't see what all the fuss was about. Tradition, loyalty to the past meant little to them. Even his wife, who was closer to him than any living being, couldn't understand. She was, after all, not a Southerner.

The Little Rock Ministerial Alliance expressed no opinion. While the school board worked out a plan, they agreed, it was better to leave the subject of integration alone.

After more than two years the school board announced its plan frankly designed "to provide as little integration spread over as long a period as legally possible." They proposed to admit a few selected students to Central High School and work down, adding every year a handful of qualified Negro children, grade by grade.

No one was satisfied. The White Citizens' Council, which editor Ashmore had termed a "manicured Ku Klux Klan," cried "Treason!" The silent majority kept its silence like prisoners in separate cells. The Negroes, bitterly disappointed, saw that real change would not come of itself.

Dunbar Ogden, at the right, with other religious leaders.

For another year the question of token integration moved back and forth through the courts. Little Rock asked for delay. In April 1957, the Supreme Court handed down its ruling. The Little Rock plan—which meant the admission of only a few Negro students to one high school and none in lower schools—was declared sufficient to satisfy the law, but it could be put off no longer.

The National Association for the Advancement of Colored

People had a strong, active branch in Little Rock under the leadership of Daisy Bates, a writer and wife of the editor of the local Negro newspaper. Quietly, efficiently, in the spring of 1957, Mrs. Bates explained to Negro parents the steps that had to be taken, the dangers, the risks, in carrying through even this small step toward freedom.

Of the sixty Negro children who asked to be enrolled in Central High, it was announced that nine had qualified. But even this gesture at desegregation was too much for the die-hards. They had no intention of permitting even one non-Caucasian student to pass through the portals of the largest school in the city.

White ministers, talking among themselves, were concerned about community tensions. When Dunbar Ogden was elected head of the Ministerial Alliance, he suggested that it might be a good idea to get together with the Negro ministerial alliance to try to build some bridge of understanding. However, there was a conference of Southern governors going on. It was felt that a meeting with Negroes at this time would merely stir up trouble.

Governor Faubus returned from the conference in July, predicting violence and bloodshed if integration was attempted at Central High. In August, a white parent petitioned the State Court to halt the admission of the nine Negro students. Faubus again testified that bloodshed was likely. And the Arkansas court agreed not to permit any integration this term. With weary determination, the NAACP lawyers announced that they would appeal again to the Federal District Court on behalf of the nine.

Just last week Dunbar Ogden had read the names of the students in his morning paper: *Elizabeth Eckford, Carlotta Walls, Minnie Jean Brown, Gloria Ray, Thelma Mothershed, Melba Patillo, Jefferson Thomas, Terence Roberts, Ernest Green.*

Six girls, three boys. Nothing in their names to show their color. If the list had been in the social columns, they might have been "among those present" at a birthday party. Or the members of the debating society David had belonged to at Central High.

For some strange reason he had thought of Enoch—Enoch, with his long, thin, brown legs, slowing down so he wouldn't win. "It's not fair!" Dunbar spoke out loud and his wife looked up from her book in surprise. "It's not right," he had said. "They've waited too long for justice. Time is of value only if it's put to some use."

He threw down the paper. In his study he began work on Sunday's sermon. Thinking of the nine dark-skinned children whose names he had already forgotten, he chose as his text: *Blessed are they who are persecuted for righteousness' sake, for theirs is the kingdom of heaven.*

After church one of the elders came to shake his hand. "I just wish the Supreme Court judges up in Washington could have heard you, Mr. Ogden. Maybe they'd stop persecutin' the South!"

The man was gone before Dunbar found the right words to explain that it was the Negroes he had in mind.

A few days later, Judge Davies of the Federal District Court overturned the State Court's decision and ordered the nine children admitted to Central High.

On the day before classes were to begin, in spite of the fact that the mayor of Little Rock said no violence was threatened, Governor Faubus called out 270 National Guardsmen "to maintain order." Excitement swept over the little city. The real mission of the troops was to *prevent* the enrollment of the nine Negro students.

Then Judge Davies had ordered the school officials to disregard the troops and permit the Negroes to attend school.

It was at this point that Mrs. Bates called Dunbar Henry

Ogden, Jr., on the phone to request him to accompany the children on their walk to school.

"I don't know," Dunbar had said at the supper table. He paced the floor half the night, but next morning he still had not made up his mind where his duty lay.

"At least I can go talk to them," he said to his wife.

As he left the house, the eight o'clock newscaster on the radio was describing the mobs gathering outside the school. But his own street was quiet. He had phoned several other ministers, and a couple had said they'd think it over. Probably neither one would show up. He walked alone, unaware that David was following half a block behind. Alone he approached the corner where Mrs. Bates had said the children were to meet. From here they would walk together to the school. Soldiers with bayonets waited to bar their way.

Dunbar Ogden ran over in his mind the things he would say. Wouldn't it be best to advise them to give up the unequal struggle, at least for the present? Why insist on the letter of the law? Yet who could deny that enforced segregation because of race, creed or color is against all Christian principles?

Dunbar counted three boys in suits and ties and five young girls in skirts and blouses seated together on a long bench. A little apart, several men and a woman waited. The parents? No. Mrs. Bates had said the school superintendent had advised the children to come alone. The man on the corner looked white—yes, he was. Reverend Will Campbell, a visitor from Nashville. One slender, business-like woman came forward. That would be Mrs. Bates.

"Reverend Ogden? It was good of you to come." She shook his outstretched hand.

Dunbar looked toward the children again. "I thought there were to be nine," he said.

"Elizabeth Eckford lives across town. I couldn't reach her last night. She'll come on the bus." It occurred to him that Mrs. Bates looked worried.

"Would you like to say a few words to the students, Reverend Ogden, before you start?"

"Before I—" Dunbar paused. He had come to talk things over, not to act. He hoped that no one took his presence here as a commitment.

He began to speak to the children, telling them how much he admired their courage, warning them against possible violence, taking a share of the blame for letting this situation come to pass. He tried to explain his own position and the position of the majority of citizens, who, though they might not desire desegregated schools, yet believed in justice and right.

"Reverend Ogden." A man's voice interrupted him. "Are you or are you not going to walk with these children?" The tone was clipped and abrupt—definitely not that usually employed by a Negro to a white in the South. Certainly not to a grandson of the Dunbars and the Ogdens of Mississippi.

Dunbar stiffened.

Then Mrs. Bates spoke softly. "What Reverend Lawrence means is, we'd feel better if you went along, Reverend Ogden."

The fear that Dunbar himself felt was mirrored in the woman's eyes. Fear of the situation . . . fear above all for the children.

"If it will make you feel better . . ." To bring comfort to another human being—this duty Dunbar responded to. "Yes," he said with a sigh. "Yes, I will go."

Two Negro ministers, the eight young people, the stranger from Nashville and Dunbar Ogden stepped off the curb. David was waiting beside a police car. The police would give protection to this point. No farther. Near him stood a thin man with glasses. Dunbar Ogden had met him once or twice. Lorch was the name. He had cousins in Natchez. A bright young man, but a radical. He was sorry to see that David seemed to be striking up an acquaintance. The two young

Elizabeth Eckford walks alone amid jeering whites as she tries to enter Central High School in Little Rock, Arkansas.

men fell easily into step and Dunbar recovered his pride and joy in his tall, blond son.

The block was short and slightly uphill. A crowd of hate-filled faces lined the way, and ahead beyond a clump of trees were the National Guard with their guns. All to keep nine Negro young people out of school! When they came to the school, Dunbar Ogden was short of breath as if he had climbed a mountain. Across the street a dark-skinned girl stood alone in a white, stiff-starched dress, surrounded by a jeering crowd of whites.

"That's Elizabeth Eckford," the child beside him whispered.

Strangely Dunbar did not feel as sorry for Elizabeth as for the soldiers with their glittering bayonets, for he knew at last that she was wholly on the side of right, and they were wrong. He watched Elizabeth Eckford make her way to a bus-stop bench. Even at this distance he could see that she was crying. A man leaned over and spoke to her and she raised her head and brushed away the tears. A white woman came out of the hooting crowd and sat down quietly beside the girl. A newspaper photographer stepped up and snapped a picture. When Dunbar saw it in the paper that night, he read the name of the woman in the caption. The woman was the wife of Lee Lorch and a Yankee. Too bad she couldn't have been somebody Southern!

How long had he known that segregation was wrong? Had the truth begun to sink in years ago, in Staunton? Or before that? Long before . . . *"You're crazier 'n a grasshopper! Snowball's my boy!"* A childish voice came to him above the shouts and clamor. But Enoch was nobody's boy. He belonged to himself and to the fellowship of us all here on this earth. And it wasn't right for him to lose those races. . . . Dunbar wished he could tell Jim. And the janitor at Davidson. He wished he could tell Reverend Lee. But if white and Negro can only go to school together, then each group may give what

it has to give, each giving and sharing on God's green earth.
. . . Dunbar Ogden, standing at the brow of the little hill,
saw not a mob of hate-torn faces, but a vision of a world rich
with fellowship.

"We'd better turn back now, Reverend." The clipped, deep
tone of the Negro minister's voice now sounded comforting
to Dunbar—sure and strong and warm.

The white Southerner and the black looked each other in
the eyes. "You lead the way, Reverend Lawrence. I'll follow,"
Dunbar said cheerfully, as friend to friend.

As they started down the hill, one of the children touched
Ogden's arm.

"Elizabeth Eckford's mother gave her a verse from the
Bible to say so she wouldn't be afraid. Do you think that's
a good idea, Reverend? For when we come back tomorrow?"

"Yes, I do, Carlotta." He knew their names now. He would
never forget them again. "I'll give you one: *The stone that the
builder rejected shall become the chief cornerstone.*"

But they did not come back the next day—Faubus' bayonets
prevented the children from entering the school for three
weeks.

The phone was already ringing when David and his father
opened the front door. Newspaper reporters, trustees of the
church, shrill-voiced women of his congregation. Threats,
pleadings, an occasional word of hesitant praise came over
the wires.

With that short uphill walk, the minister of the Central
Presbyterian Church had become a leading spokesman for
integration in Little Rock.

Three weeks later, the President of the United States at
last used his authority to open the doors for the Negroes. The
same threat of force that Faubus had employed to bar their
entrance was now employed to protect them. For months
soldiers kept watch. Charges, counter-charges troubled the

town. Crosses were burned. Bombs were thrown. Through it all the nine young people stayed in school.

Dunbar Ogden was able to bring together a small group of white and black citizens to discuss their mutual concerns, to know one another slightly and to unite in a common goal of peace with justice.

A few of his congregation became part of the group. But not enough were on his side to keep him from being dismissed from his church. Daisy Bates and her husband lost their newspaper.

Three months before the end of the tumultuous school year, on his last night in Little Rock, Dunbar Ogden left the Manse and took a walk alone in a drizzling February rain. His footsteps led him up the rise to Central High. It had seemed so steep that first day—you'd hardly call it a hill at all—but nine Negro children had made this particular spot their own—theirs and in small way, his.

The struggle for acceptance of an integrated school was not over. Little Rock had much "unfinished business" in which he would have no further share. He had accepted his dismissal from the church as a small price to pay for the new freedom to be himself. He would cheerfully begin again as assistant pastor in a church in West Virginia on the very border of his beloved Southland. But tonight he felt unreasonably depressed.

It was not easy for a Dunbar and an Ogden, deeply rooted in the history of the South, to hear himself called a traitor to his race, a traitor to his class. Not easy to open outraged letters from Davidson College alumni or from his own family writing from Mississippi. Not easy to leave David in Little Rock to suffer taunts and insults.

"It would have been safer to have stayed at the foot of this hill," he said to himself.

The muscles of his throat tightened as he glimpsed a burly figure in the shadow of a wall. It was not the first time he had been followed. He began to perspire and his right hand doubled of itself into a fist.

The man stepped out of the shadows and Dunbar breathed again. He could see that the man was black.

"Reverend Ogden." The voice out of the shadows was soft and with an accent very like his own. "I read where you're going away. I been wanting to tell you, it was a fine thing you did, walking up to the school with the children. But do you mind if I ask, how come you made up your mind to do it?"

Dunbar Ogden laughed. It was the laughter of a free man. "I never did make up my mind," he answered. "You might say I was pushed—by history."

# Not
# so wild
# 11 a dream

The "tender warriors" of Little Rock—the nine students who braved that first year in integrated Central High—were the vanguard of an army. The events at Little Rock and a bus boycott that had taken place just a few months before in Montgomery, Alabama, were, taken together, a turning point in Southern history. In the Little Rock episode, young people, not even out of high school, fought for their own freedom. In Montgomery, the participants in the struggle were the middle-aged and elderly walking in protest against segregation in the buses—fifty thousand of them—walking to victory though they had to walk for a solid year. The old people walked, but even then, in Montgomery, it was youth who forged for them the new and potent weapon of non-violent mass action. Youth, in the person of twenty-six-year-old Martin Luther King, Jr.

At Boston University Theological School, King had studied the teachings of Mahatma Gandhi's philosophy of non-violent protest and Thoreau's theory of civil disobedience. These ideas were blended in the young Negro minister's thinking with the teachings of Jesus. He saw non-violent protest against injustice as a potent method available to oppressed people. The success of the Montgomery boycott, the effect of the courageous stand of the Little Rock children were contagious.

Members of an NAACP Youth Group in a college for

Nonviolent protest against injustice is a potent force used by

Gandhi's followers in India and some American civil rights groups.

Negroes in Tallahassee, Florida, in 1956 started a bus boycott of their own. The arrest of young students carrying picket signs announcing the non-violent boycott brought a new factor into the movement—a white Southerner joined in.

Eighteen-year-old Richard Parker would have told anyone who asked him that Florida Negroes had nothing to complain about. He had never been interested in the "Negro problem" and was just walking along the sidewalk where the picketers were being put under arrest. With the usual contempt of the white police for Negroes, the officers were pushing the students around. Parker was struck perhaps by the dignity of the victims, or he may have stopped simply out of curiosity.

A policeman looked with sudden suspicion at the lanky red-headed boy carrying books under his arm. "Are you one of 'em? Do you belong to that—NAACP?"

Richard Parker drew a deep breath. Was he one with Negroes? It was a new thought. Certainly he hated injustice. He stared at the officer. "The NAACP? I just joined."

And Parker was hauled off to jail with the rest.

In the spring of 1960, four Negro students in Greensboro, North Carolina, sat down at Woolworth's lunch counter near their segregated college campus. "What's the good of education without freedom?" they asked themselves. And freedom at this moment was the right to put your dime on the counter and be served a cup of coffee.

The Greensboro students sat quietly after they had been refused service, and sat and sat at the counter, day after day until the police came to arrest them for "disturbing the peace." Next morning ten students sat in and went to jail. Within a week the Woolworth sit-ins numbered a hundred— a mixed group, dark-skinned and fair-skinned. Several Caucasian students from the other side of town had come to take part in the demonstration against injustice. They, too, accepted beatings and prison for the sake of freedom.

The demonstrations announced the discontent with segregation. The news of the Greensboro sit-ins set off dozens of others over the South; almost every sit-in had white Southerners getting arrested alongside of Negroes. A cup of coffee became a symbol of liberty; to be jailed or spit on or beaten to suffer for freedom was to be a man. Thousands of students staged non-violent demonstrations that year. Sit-ins; wade-ins for the right to use public beaches; read-ins in public white-only libraries; kneel-ins on the steps of the all-white churches . . . Every challenge was a stick of dynamite to explode the racist myth of white superiority, the pretense that Negroes were contented with things the way they were.

Freedom Rides followed the sit-ins with more arrests and increasing mob violence. Every outrage brought new whites into the movement. Northerners were aroused, especially those of Southern background, because they knew what courage and sacrifice any protest in the Southern states demanded.

Mississippi-born William Moore was a white postman living in Maryland. He decided to walk the length of the country to deliver a letter to Governor Barnett of Mississippi, a plea for freedom and understanding of the plight of the Negroes in Mississippi. Moore was not a young man but he had the faith of youth. He wore a placard on his walk announcing his destination and purpose. Through Virginia, through the Carolinas and Georgia, he met with expected jeers and was pelted with clods of earth and rocks. As he crossed the line into Alabama, William Moore was shot and killed.

The contents of the undelivered letter were widely read and came to the notice of a young man in college in Alabama, Sam Shiran, determined to take up the dead postman's walk. He was joined by white and Negro students who had conducted non-violent demonstrations in Nashville, Tennessee. When Sam Shiran re-entered his native state of Alabama, he was arrested and carted off to jail. The governor of Mississippi never got Moore's letter, but the non-violent resistance movement had acquired a new recruit.

The Student Non-violent Coordinating Committee was organized before the year was over. SNCC was based on Dr. King's philosophy, but it was independent—youth's challenge to the future. At their organizing conference in Atlanta, a fifth of the students were white, most of them from Southern "white" colleges.

"Not enough," Mrs. Baker, their adult adviser commented.

Recruits were needed from among the silent, the uncommitted Southerners. In a democracy, numbers count. "No white person in the South can afford to be neutral," she said.

Dozens of young white students heard the message and responded. One of the first to come forward was the son of a minister who had been attending a small Methodist college in Montgomery. "Where is tomorrow born? Where does the future start?" Robert Zellner's precarious future started in the Montgomery courthouse where he had gone in order to get material for a term paper and happened to listen to Martin Luther King's trial in a suit that grew out of the Montgomery bus boycott.


> Now speak up, Justice, and state your case
> Are you now
> Or have you ever been
> A member of
> The human race?


William Moore was killed on his lonely walk through the South pleading for the rights of American Negroes.

# Robert Zellner

The meeting of SNCC workers in McComb, Mississippi, had been going on all morning in the cluttered loft that served as office and general work room for the six-member staff. The Negroes, except two, were from the immediate area, one of the girls a sharecropper's daughter. The young man with a hat on had taught for a year in a country school. The other girl and the short stocky youth with dark glasses had spent a year at college before they gave up to join SNCC. They had been working in McComb many weeks on a voter registration campaign. Across the table sat dark husky Charles McDew, chairman of SNCC, and Robert Moses. The project to encourage the disfranchised Negroes of McComb to register was Moses' idea. He had spent a year planning, laying a foundation. He was a Harvard-trained teacher from New York, a man with a long vision. His campaign required careful preparation, first to find people to register who felt able to take the risk of going to the courthouse to apply—the risk of being put off their land or losing jobs—or worse. Then he prepared those with sufficient education to pass the registration tests set up by the state, not for the purpose of finding qualified voters but to bar even the best qualified from the privilege of casting his vote. For the illiterate, SNCC workers had to set up classes in reading and writing and on the discipline of non-violent resistance when violence was visited on them.

The seventh person at the rough pine-board table knew in general what went on in voter registration drives. He was Robert Zellner, recently appointed field secretary to work among white students, to inform them of the struggle going on around them which they would never see mentioned in the papers they read, to inspire them if possible to join in the long struggle ahead. To do this job, Bob Zellner felt he must know what was being done in various localities, so he attended as many planning sessions in as many places as possible.

"But never one like this," he thought, shifting his position a little, stretching his long legs under the table. He was tall. Taller than any of his anxious-faced colleagues in the room. His deep-set eyes fastened on a church spire visible through the window. It glistened white against a hazy September sky— like a picture on a Sunday school card that might be given out to the children. A "white" church, Bob guessed, since it was so nicely painted. Was it the one that E. H. Hurst, member of the Mississippi legislature, went to when he was electioneering in McComb? Hurst was the man who was said to have fired the shot that killed Herbert Lee. Lee was a farmer who dared raise his voice for just treatment for himself and for his fellow Negroes.

The murder had not occurred in McComb but in Liberty, the next town, where Lee had gone with a load of cotton to be ginned. "Shot in self-defense" had been the coroner's verdict just ten days ago. The verdict was given, the murderer free on bail while the body still lay in the road.

Self-defense, though Lee had not possessed a weapon of any kind—much less the one the sheriff claimed he found under his dead hand . . . Lewis Allen and two other Negro witnesses had been forced to give false testimony about the pistol. Hurst had been acquitted just yesterday. . . . Allen was going to the FBI to tell them the truth about the murder.

Bob Moses had told Zellner all the details when he got to McComb a couple of hours before. The local SNCC workers had tightened up at first, seeing Moses bring a white boy to their meeting. Every white person they had ever known in this fear-ridden county had been an enemy. But two hours and the confidence they had in Moses had quieted their distrust. They looked Bob Zellner in the eyes now and liked what they saw.

"It was self-defense, all right," the stout girl in the flowered dress said. "Herbert had been studying the Constitution real hard for his voter's test. If he'd made it—him and a few thousand like him, they could've voted Mr. Hurst right out of his job in the legislature."

"Well, like I said at the protest meeting last night," someone commented, "I lost my job and I didn't think it was necessary to kill anybody over it."

That was the nearest they came to talking about registration. Everybody was too full of the murder of Herbert Lee. They told Zellner about the mass meeting held the night of the killing and again last night. They talked of the spirit of the people, how tired they were of murders in broad daylight and nobody ever punished. No white men. They were tired, too, of discrimination and were ready to turn the state upside down with demonstrations. The high school students planned to walk out of school after lunch to protest in front of the courthouse.

About one o'clock in the afternoon, the talk was interrupted by the strange, far-off sound of tramping feet. Through the open window, Zellner began to hear faint words of "We Shall Overcome." There was a rush to the window. Watching over the heads of the others, Bob waited for the arrival of the high school procession. Finally he saw it, a long thin line: one hundred and twenty students who had walked out of school. They had appointed line captains and had printed posters: *Lee Could Be Me. America, Help Us. We Want to Be Free.*

The SNCC workers dashed down to join the column. Bob started to follow, then he hesitated. He was the only white person there and he debated with himself. "If I go, there may be more violence than there would otherwise be. Being the only white man may cause the violence to be directed at me. My parents will suffer by losing their jobs, and besides I'm supposed to work just with white students and if I get involved here, my effectiveness in SNCC may be impaired."

These were all good reasons to stay behind and let the students face Mississippi by themselves. Bob suddenly realized that everyone who had faced the decision to stand up and be counted in any struggle had to face some kind of questions. Quietly he walked down the steps and took his place in line to march to the courthouse.

The march was uneventful until they reached the center of town, where a man drove his car straight at the line. He crashed through. Several of the young people just managed to jump out of the way. Then the man leaped out of his car and attacked one of the boys with an iron wrench. The boy stood motionless and took the blow. A few drops of blood oozed from his broken skin. Unable to start trouble, the infuriated man stalked to his car and drove away.

Near the courthouse, Bob was startled to hear his name shouted. "Zellner, I'm going to get you." He recognized the red, distorted face leaning out of the car. It was a classmate from Huntingdon College! The car disappeared and Bob saw

and heard a screaming mob surrounding the steps of the courthouse, waiting for the marchers. Somehow a lane was opened and the first column reached the step. The leader moved to the step just above and attempted, above the howls, to lead the group in prayer. A policeman at the door stepped down, grabbed him by the shoulder and arrested him. Another took his place and knelt to pray. He, too, was arrested.

The whole line was ordered into the building, but when it was Bob Zellner's turn to enter, the chief of police held him back. Five or six men rushed up and began beating him. McDew and Moses were just behind and tried to make a shield against the blows by interposing their own bodies. They were dragged away by police. From the steps came a booted kick in Zellner's face. He fell, unconscious.

When he regained consciousness he was in a car with six men in shirt sleeves, riding through open country. He could see cars ahead and see others following. He huddled in a corner, still dizzy, and took time to think things over. He was convinced that he was going to die, but he did not regret what he had chosen to do. He wouldn't have exchanged places with any one of the bitter, frustrated men in the car. From the fragments of talk he overheard, the plan was for another carful to overtake them. Men who had not been seen anywhere near City Hall would do the killing.

But the plan somehow misfired. The driver turned the car back and forth on country lanes until dark and then, tired of waiting for a car that didn't come, dumped Bob into the jail at Magnolia, a few miles from McComb.

Zellner wasn't charged with any crime or given a chance to get in touch with a lawyer. He was simply pushed into a solitary cell without food or bedding and locked in for the night.

Robert Zellner plays cards with students at a "freedom school" in Oxford, Mississippi.

Stretched out on the clammy floor, unable to sleep, he let pictures of home drift through his mind. Not any special house, because they had lived in so many parsonages all through his boyhood that none ever seemed a real home. Home was not rooms and furniture. It was not even the sandy soil of the Gulf Coast of Alabama. Home for Bob Zellner was his spritely, energetic mother and country-preacher father with the voice of a prophet and the twinkle in his eyes of a mischievous boy. Just those two—not his four brothers, not his uncles and aunts and grandparents. Just Dad and Mom—they were his roots—his home.

His father was a Methodist minister and the Conference made a point of moving him to a different church every three years. The churches and parsonages had almost always been in small, out-of-the-way places in south Alabama, around Mobile. Even the church in Mobile which his father presided over during Bob's years of high school was on the edge of town, on the wrong side of the tracks.

The Reverend Zellner was a fine preacher and a wonderful man. The reason he never was made the minister of one of the big brownstone churches in Mobile or Birmingham or Montgomery was because of his ideas. He really believed in brotherhood and speaking with respect to colored people even if he didn't have an opportunity to know any except an occasional maid. He stood up for union labor and, more distressing still, spoke out in Conference for Bishop Oxnam, whom Senator McCarthy had called a "Red."

Bob's mother was proud of the stand her husband had taken. She didn't mind that it meant living in inconvenient parsonages with old-fashioned iceboxes instead of an electric refrigerator and not having a radio or TV. She had brought

Martin Luther King leads Negroes and whites in a "freedom march."

up her five sons not to mind either and (the gentlest soul on earth) had not hesitated to urge them to fight back when gangs in the neighborhood in every new town tested the courage of the minister's sons. But that was before the days of Dr. King's non-violent resistance movement. Mrs. Zellner had read everything she could find about his philosophy, even before Bob went to work for SNCC.

Bob realized when he talked to other white SNCC workers how fortunate he was to have parents who approved of what he was doing. That was one of the hardest things in the South, the way disagreement about segregation broke up families. Many more young people would be in the movement, he felt, if they weren't held back by a mother or father who wanted to keep the Negro in his traditional place. Even in his own family there was grandfather Zellner in Birmingham and two uncles—all Klansman and outraged that Bob was bringing disgrace on the Zellner name by associating with colored people.

The young man sat up abruptly in the bleak darkness of the jail cell. What if his father hadn't changed! He, too, had been high up in the Klan when he was Bob's age. Suppose his father and mother had clung to their bigoted ideas—would *he* be working for freedom and brotherhood today?

"But for them, I could have grown up hating like those men in the car hate. Holding back with baseball bats and guns the better world that's coming." His parents in their youth had made the break with the slave-ridden past that he was asking others to make today.

A few days later, while they were both in separate jails, Bob had a letter from Robert Moses. Most of the letter was about what the lawyers were doing to arrange bail, or to try to set an early date for the trial and start the appeals under way. It was a foregone conclusion that the SNCC workers would be found guilty of "disturbing the peace" or "conspiracy to start a riot." Whatever the charge, Moses wrote, a Negro or anyone on his side is always guilty in the eyes of a Mississippi judge.

Then he had added at the bottom of the letter:

> Your presence has had an effect on the young Mississippians. They had never known a sympathetic white person before. The kids here had said, "We won't have anything to do with peckerwoods (meaning white people). But now since Bob Zellner demonstrated with us and was beaten, we believe that maybe there are some good white people after all.

When he got out of jail a week later, Zellner sent the letter to his mother and father, "Because," he said to himself, "it really belongs to them."

The example and support Bob Zellner received from his parents were a tremendous source of his strength. It made things easier for him to *live* what he believed than for many of his white colleagues. But this doesn't tell the whole story. His college days are important too.

He had attended Huntingdon College, a Methodist school in Montgomery. The bus boycott had just come to its victorious end when he entered Huntingdon. Bob had been mildly pleased that the Negroes had won, because it didn't seem right for them to have to sit in the back of the buses if they didn't want to. He didn't like to see people abused and have their feelings hurt. However, the bus boycott was just something he read about in the newspapers. He didn't understand its great significance until later.

It was something that happened to one of the professors that eventually pushed Bob to take an active stand for integration. A popular young art professor had attended a few integrated meetings at the nearby college for Negroes. After one of these gatherings, he offered to drive a Negro student home and the boy sat beside him in the front seat of the car. For this the professor was arrested and charged with disorderly conduct. The president of the college was furious— not at the unfairness of such bigotry, but at the professor for associating with colored people. He "accepted" his resignation and refused even to let him enter the campus grounds to remove his personal belongings.

Even though the professor had been head of the art department which he had built up from nothing and had done all the art work for the yearbook, his picture and his name were stricken from it. His name was also blotted out from the program of a play he had been directing in which Bob took a leading role.

To see men (the president and the administrators of the school) take such action made the sensitive boy realize what a radical evil racism was and to make up his mind that "radical evil can only be destroyed by radical action." He got some of his classmates to go with him to the president to protest the injustice, but protest was useless. As far as Huntingdon was concerned the art professor's career was ended—all because he had given a Negro a ride in his car.

Bob didn't know any Negroes in Montgomery himself and he didn't try to, until near the close of his senior year. He had been assigned a term paper: "The racial problem and your solution to it." Instead of just going to the library to read a couple of books, he decided to go down to the courthouse to attend a Federal hearing where several Negro ministers as well as the publishers of The New York Times were being charged with libel by Montgomery officials. The suit concerned an ad published in defense of Reverend Martin Luther King, Jr., and signed by the ministers during the bus boycott. Bob was greatly impressed with the testimony of Reverend Abernathy and the witty young minister from Birmingham, Reverend Fred Shuttlesworth, and greatly moved by the eloquent words spoken by King.

On the second day of the trial he brought three of his friends along and they sat on the side of the courtroom reserved for Negroes until the bailiff forced them to move. The city officials were awarded large damages at the close of the hearing, and Abernathy's car and also Shuttlesworth's were promptly confiscated in partial payment. (The decision of the Montgomery judge failed to stand up in the higher courts but the long drawn-out action which was two years old served its purpose. It was intended as a warning to anyone fighting for civil rights.) The effect on Bob Zellner was to arouse admiration and sympathy for the Negroes. He and his friends spoke briefly with them as they were leaving the court. Bob was observed shaking their hands.

As a result of the stir the handshakes caused, the students were sharply reprimanded. Bob was called to the office of the state attorney general and warned against committing such a breach of etiquette in the future because it was well known that Communists were behind the "integration men." Two crosses were burned under Bob's dormitory window and the college president asked Bob and his friends to sign a pledge that they would cease their activities or withdraw from the college.

With the backing of his parents, Bob did neither. Instead he got twenty-two students to join in sending a letter to the ministers expressing their regret over the action of the city officials. They enclosed twenty-two dollars as "a token of moral support." A more serious offense in the eyes of the authorities was the weekend Bob spent at Highlander with many integration leaders.

The college year was so near its end that the administration

A group of whites had followed the bus containing "freedom fire, attacking the passengers as they fled.

riders." They stoned the bus and slashed its tires, then set it on

awarded Bob his degree anyhow. The president was probably glad to get such a troublesome student safely away from Huntingdon!

Immediately after graduation Bob enrolled in a non-violent workshop at Reverend Abernathy's church with students from the Negro college. It was the year of the sit-ins, and the Negro students were preparing to demonstrate in the state capital. Their reasoning was that the capital cafeteria was supported in part by the taxes Negro citizens paid, and that they therefore should be allowed to buy a cup of coffee at the counter like other taxpaying citizens. The high spirits of the Negro demonstrators—singing as they marched, though they were risking expulsion from school and arrest and jail—delighted Bob. It promised to be quite a summer!

But then came tragedy when Freedom Riders came to Montgomery and were met by a riotous mob. The first Freedom bus had been burned in Anniston. The riders had met with violence in Birmingham and been forced to fly to New Orleans without being able to test accommodations. Now in Montgomery a second group met with even greater violence.

When he heard the news of the riot, Bob Zellner ran down to the bus station to see if he could be of help. The mob was by this time dispersed, the wounded Negroes in the segregated wards in the city hospital, the others sheltered in the basement of a Negro church. All that Bob saw of the violence were two smashed cameras, bits of torn clothing trampled underfoot on the sidewalk and some dark spots of dried blood.

Step by step, events such as these were drawing Bob Zellner closer to enlistment in what he likes to call Gideon's army. It was the letter he had written to the ministers from college that led to his work with SNCC. Reverend Abernathy, touched by the message, had showed it to Anne Braden, staff writer of the news monthly, the *Southern Patriot;* Mrs. Braden asked permission to print it. Of the twenty-two who had signed the letter, only Bob Zellner was willing to have his signature appear. Anne Braden made a trip from New Orleans to Montgomery to talk about the letter. As would be expected, the two crusaders for freedom became staunch friends. They shared an unswerving love for the South and faith that the wall that separates Negroes and whites would not stand forever.

After Zellner left the Mississippi jail, the Southern Conference Educational Fund, publishers of the *Southern Patriot,* made a grant of money to SNCC for Bob to work with the white Southern students. Partly because of his efforts, more and more white Southerners have taken an active part in the movement. Where one white student spoke out at Alabama University for Autherine Lucy in 1956, a dozen risked their lives to protect James Meredith at the University of Mississippi six years later. Not long after the riots which followed Meredith's admission, Bob was able to spend a week on the Mississippi campus talking to the students who had dared to defend the young Negro scholar. Bob thanked them in the name of their fellow Southerners.

But Zellner's career with SNCC was not limited to pleasant visits on Southern campuses. His progress through the South may be traced from jail to jail. After McComb came Albany, Georgia, then Baton Rouge, Louisiana, where he was charged with "criminal anarchy." Talladega, Alabama, followed. Then he returned to Montgomery to visit his old alma mater. He was walking quietly along the Huntingdon campus talking with some students when he was arrested by state troopers. The charge: vagrancy. During the brutal repression of student demonstrations in Danville, Virginia, in the summer of 1963, Bob was arrested five times.

Neither jailings nor beatings nor fire hoses altered his indomitable determination. Through it all the full support of his family showed itself by public statements, pamphlets and articles. They attended his trials and cheerfully bore the brunt of newspaper notoriety and harassment.

Bob had barely recovered from the injuries received at Danville before the date set for his wedding to Dorothy Miller of New York. Dorothy had come South to work in the SNCC headquarters in Atlanta. There was too much going that summer for the two young crusaders to plan a formal wedding. They were married in Atlanta, by a Negro minister. A new form of civil disobedience, since it is against Georgia law for a white couple to stand before a Negro minister to take their marriage vows!

At the time of their wedding, the Zellners looked back at the two years they had given to the struggle. Bob had twelve convictions for an assortment of "crimes" he was charged with. Fines levied against him amounted to $20,000. The cases were all appealed and by 1965 the convictions had been set aside. Once again, in 1967, with courage reinforced by experience, Bob and Dorothy Zellner are working in the South. They are looking forward toward a future when white and black will have the power to achieve their common needs.

"Slogans like *democracy* and *equality* and *brotherhood* are fine in their place but they don't solve practical everyday problems and they are not going to solve the Negro problem," a state senator from Georgia said.

Robert Zellner's answer was, "Gideon's army is growing larger, and through its strength I do believe that we will be able to post proof that brotherhood is not so wild a dream."

# Bibliography

# Bibliography

A great deal has been written about the South and about the condition of the Negro people by Negroes themselves. Very little has been written about white dissenters from the *status quo*. The list below is made up chiefly of works that I read in connection with the research for my book, although the most valuable sources are omitted, namely the old newspapers and records in historical society journals.

Aptheker, Herbert, *Documentary History of the Negro People in the United States*. New York: Citadel Press, 1951.

Aptheker, Herbert, *Negro Slave Revolts in the United States*. New York: International, 1939.

Beecher, John, *To Live and Die in Dixie*. Birmingham: Red Mountain Press, 1966.

Belfrage, Cedric, *A Faith To Free the People*. New York: Dryden Press, 1944.

Blackford, L. Minor, *Mine Eyes Have Seen the Glory*. Cambridge: Harvard University Press, 1954.

Bontemps, Arna, and Hughes, Langston, *Poetry of the Negro*. New York: Doubleday, 1949.

Braden, Anne, *The Wall Between*. New York: Monthly Review Press, 1958.

Buckmaster, Henrietta, *Let My People Go*. Boston: Beacon Press; Garden City: Doubleday, 1941.

Cable, George W., *The Silent South*. New York: Scribner, 1962.

Cash, J. W., *The Mind of the South*. New York: Knopf, 1941.

Coffin, Levi, *Reminiscences of Levi Coffin*. Cincinnati: Western Tract Society, 1876.

Douglass, Frederick, *Life and Times of Frederick Douglass*. New York: Collier, 1883.

DuBois, W. E. B., *Black Reconstruction*. New York: Harcourt, Brace, 1935.

DuBois, W. E. B., *John Brown*. New York: International, 1962.

Embree, Edwin, *Thirteen Against the Odds*. New York: Houghton Mifflin, 1960.

Foner, Philip, ed., *Basic Writings of Thomas Jefferson*. New York: Wiley Book Company, 1944.

Freeman, Douglas Southall, *George Washington*. New York: Scribner, 1948.

Griffin, John Howard, *Black Like Me*. New York: Houghton Mifflin, 1960.

Hughes, Langston, *Fight for Freedom*. New York: Berkeley Press, 1962.

Phillips, Ulrich B., *Life and Labor in the Old South*. Boston: Little Brown, 1929.

Sherman, W. T., *Memoirs: William Tecumseh Sherman*. New York: Webster, 1891.

Thomas, B. P., *Theodore Weld, Crusader for Freedom*. New Brunswick, N.J.: Rutgers University Press, 1950.

Thomas, G. H. T., *Memoirs of Major General George H. Thomas*. Philadelphia: Lippincott, 1881.

Townsend, Sara Bertha, *An American Soldier: John Laurens*. Raleigh, N.C.: Edwards and Broughton, 1958.

Turner, Ailin, ed., *The Negro Question*. Garden City, N.Y.: Doubleday, 1958.

Wakefield, Dan, *Revolt in the South*. New York: Grove, 1960.

Woodward, C. Vann, *The Strange Career of Jim Crow*. New York: Oxford, 1956.

Zinn, Howard, *The New Abolitionists*. Boston: Beacon, 1964.

# Index

# Index